BROADCAST COPYWRITING AS PROCESS

Developed under the
advisory editorship of
Thomas W. Bohn, Dean
School of Communications,
Ithaca College

BROADCAST COPYWRITING AS PROCESS

A PRACTICAL APPROACH TO COPYWRITING FOR RADIO AND TELEVISION

J. Clark Weaver

Florida State University

Longman

New York & London

BROADCAST COPYWRITING AS PROCESS
A Practical Approach to Copywriting for
Radio and Television

Longman Inc., 1560 Broadway, New York, N.Y. 10036
Associated companies, branches, and representatives
throughout the world.

Developmental Editor: Gordon T. R. Anderson
Editorial and Design Supervisor: James Fields
Production/Manufacturing: Ferne Y. Kawahara
Composition: Graphicraft Typesetters
Printing and Binding: Malloy Lithographing Inc.

Library of Congress Cataloging in Publication Data

Weaver, J. Clark.
  Broadcast copywriting as process.

  Includes index.
  1. Advertising copy.   2. Broadcast advertising.
I. Title.
HF5825.W38   1984   659.14   83-19953
ISBN 0-582-28456-2

Manufactured in the United States of America
Printing: 9 8 7 6 5 4 3 2 1   Year: 92 91 90 89 88 87 86 85 84

Contents

PART II: WRITING

How to Write the Dramatic Commercial:
The Five-Step Process   104
Assignments: The Five-Step Dramatic Commercial   116

PART III: REWRITING

Chapter 7
Rewriting   119

Preface

Many young people want a career in broadcast copywriting. Most of those who apply for a job report the same problem. Without previous experience they get no job, and without a job they get no experience. But even without experience most report they have no problem when their resume indicates, or they demonstrate, that they can write.

The purpose of this textbook is to help beginners learn how to write copy. Experiential evidence indicates that one can learn to write just as one can learn to drive a car. Naturally some learn to write sooner just as some learn to drive sooner. In general, how soon and how well each person learns depends on persistence and a willingness to follow instructions.

Almost all human accomplishments are achieved by following some form of process. As an approach to learning, a process is a practical way to set an action in motion and continue it to a conclusion. For example, a factory assembly line is a process, calling football signals is a process, and so is a recipe for baking a cake.

Learning time is shortened when a process is followed. Ask any professional—a musician, golfer, surgeon, gymnast, or whomever. Each will tell you that developing skill is a prerequisite to success.

This text is divided into three parts to help beginning writers gain essential skills. Part I is called Prewriting. The first three chapters give the writer a workable understanding of commercial broadcast communicating. Understanding the content of these three chapters helps the writer learn how to motivate listener-viewers. Chapter 4 introduces the writer to the different kinds of commercials.

Part II, Writing, shows the individual *how* to write commercial copy.

The six-step, seven-step, and five-step processes serve this purpose.

Part III, Rewriting, is concerned with perfecting what has been written. The writer is introduced to professional rewriting techniques.

Understanding how to communicate, how to get ready to write, how to write, and then how to rewrite is the way to develop self-confidence. Psychological research indicates that when a person attempts to create a technique without following a process, feelings of guilt and frustration about not being able to live up to one's expectations usually get in the way of achievement. These feelings about writing are normal. They occur because most of us think of writing as an accomplishment available only to those with special talents. We overlook the fact that by following a process, writing can be learned.

As you follow the procedures and processes in this text, remember that the more disciplined you are, the sooner you will be able to write copy. Euclid once said, "There is no royal road to geometry." This is also true of learning how to write commercial copy. Nonetheless, persistent use of the processes in this text will make learning this skill easier. Furthermore, knowing how to write will help you get a broadcast job much sooner.

For feedback and contributions to the concept of this text, my special thanks to Thomas W. Bohn, Dean, School of Communications, Ithaca College; Theodore Clevenger, Jr., Dean, College of Communication, Florida State University; Joseph C. Walters, Department of Communication, University of Texas, El Paso; Woodrow Wirsig, formerly Editor Printers Ink, President of Better Business Bureau Metropolitan New York; Edward J. Forrest, College of Communication, Florida State University; George P. Wilson, Director, Telecommunicative Arts, Iowa State University; Executive Editor Gordon T. R. Anderson, production editor James Fields, and editorial assistant Veta Maillard; and especially to Inez K. at home.

PART I

PREWRITING

CHAPTER 1

Broadcast Copywriting: A Communication Process

COMMUNICATION AS PROCESS

The concept that communication is a process was advanced by Claude E. Shannon and Warren Weaver. These two mathematicians first developed this communication theory in an effort to improve electronic signal channeling from a specific source to a specific receiver. The explanation of their theory as it relates to communication was published in 1949 by the University of Illinois Press under the title *The Mathematical Theory of Communication*.

Since that time, their theory has been described, researched, diagramed, restructured, and augmented in many ways. The concept has also been adapted and adjusted to include all forms of human communication. As a result, their basic concept and theory is now applicable to radio and television copywriting. That is why every individual who wishes to write radio and television commercials must first understand their concept.

As we all know, person-to-person communication is a two-way process. Someone talks or signals, and someone hears or sees and then interprets the message. The person who receives and interprets the

3

message then reacts or responds to the person who is the source of the message.

Fundamentally, all human communication is a process whether it is audible, visible, or a combination of the two. Moreover, communication has five basic steps. There is the *source*, the person initiating the message; the *message*, that which is being communicated; the *channel*, the person's voice or sign symbols; the *receiver*, the person(s) seeing or hearing the message; and the *feedback*, the receiver's response to the source's message.

To illustrate these five steps and show how each functions, let us apply them to a home situation. Suppose a father, the *source*, calls, *channels* with his voice to his son John, the *receiver*, the following *message*: "John! Be sure your dog is in the basement tonight. The temperature will drop to thirty degrees."

John, the receiver, has had experience with temperatures, an experience that is now a frame of reference that reinforces his response. Therefore, his interpretation of the message is that a clear and present danger exists and that he needs to get the dog into the warm basement. John's frame of reference, responsible for his current interpretation of the message, is that his first dog was left out in the cold, became ill, and died. Because of this frame of reference, John's reply, *feedback* to his father, the source, is, "Okay, Dad!"

Note the five logical communication steps: *source*, the father; *message*, what the father said; *channel*, the father's voice; *receiver*, son John; *feedback*, what John said to his father.

Most person-to-person message exchanges cannot be diagramed as easily as the example here because the communication process is not always limited to five steps. In fact, this illustration is an oversimplification. Here is why.

Other factors constantly enter into the relationships between individuals, especially the source and the receiver. Suppose that when the father calls, John does not hear, does not *receive* the message. The reason for his not receiving it is that John is in the basement with his radio turned on. His father is channeling from the hallway on the second floor. When John does not respond, the father calls again; he *channels* the *message* a second time. This time the father increases the intensity of his voice, the channel, to make sure his message gets through the noise that interferes, the music from the radio.

Also suppose that John's frame of reference linking cold weather with the death of his previous dog has been pushed aside by time and other concerns. John is older now. As a result he may no longer feel or believe that a clear and present danger exists for his dog even if the dog is left out in the cold. In other words, John is now questioning the meaning in his father's *message*.

John may also feel that his father has no right to tell him to get the dog into the basement because another of John's frames of references is telling him that the dog belongs to the entire family. It is not just John's dog. In addition, John may feel that his father is aware of his thinking.

If John's frames of reference are causing him to interpret his father's message in this manner, he is being a very normal human being. Every person has various frames of reference experiences that conflict with each message sent or received. As a result communication becomes difficult under the best of circumstances.

To help avoid such difficulties, messages should be qualified to help prevent misinterpretation. When misinterpretation occurs, message reception usually produces negative *feedback*, a negative response.

To help discover how to coordinate the communication process, let us look at two additional steps.

Encoding, Decoding

The specific nature of feedback is determined by how the receiver interprets or qualifies the received message. This process is called *decoding*.

Encoding by the source is the process of selecting, choosing, preparing, and stating appropriately the concepts and ideas included in the message.

The presence of certain frames of reference in a person's mind during encoding reflects the source's physiological, neurological, and psychological experiences. When not taken into consideration, these frames of reference are often responsible for vagueness in message content. When the content is not controlled or qualified, the frames of reference called up in the receiver frequently come in conflict with the source's intention in the message. When conflict in understanding is created by message content, the receiver's response is often at odds with the source's intention.

The frames of reference that most often interfere with the source's encoding are those that involve the individual's family, neighbors, job, age, race, health, occupation, income, social values, beliefs, religion, and other aspects of an environment that may cause personal stress-related reactions. In other words, personal stress of some kind is present in every individual and may prejudice his or her encoding or decoding.

One way to begin controlling message content so that it will not conflict with a receiver's personal stress is to think through the purpose and nature of each communication step and decide specifically how you want each step to function. Visualize each step as follows: (1) You, the *source*, (2) *encode* (3) a *message* (4) to be *channeled*, broadcast (5) to *receivers*, the listener-viewers (6) who *decode* it, interpret (7) and react with appropriate *feedback* response.

Another way to achieve a correlation between *source encoding* and *receiver decoding* is to understand your own personality dominances and then encode the message so that it is free of your personal egocentric limitations, your personal prejudices.

Developing an ability to be objective when writing a message can begin by visualizing all the possible frames of references known to 1000 listener-viewers. Remember, each listener-viewer may have a different frame of reference for each thought in the message. For example, some listener-viewers will decode a message differently, or not at all, because they are socially shy, lack skills, feel insecure, lack confidence, have a headache, are introverted, lack drive, are dominated by someone, are dependent on someone, are lacking in verbal skills. Or they are domineering, indecisive, nervous, unhappy, unrealistic, intellectual, self-conscious, aggressive, belligerent, extroverted, generous, rationalizing, cheerful, unstable, self-seeking, aloof, retiring, sexually aggressive, anxious, practical, or purposeful. Or they are dominated by a sense of power, in need of friends, feel slighted, or unaware of a sense of purpose. And there are hundreds of other dominant feelings about the *self*.

In addition to understanding how personality dominances influence the nature of feedback, the copywriter for radio and television must also learn to visualize the many confusing and distracting aspects of an environment that dominate each receiver's decoding of a message into appropriate feedback. For example, the listener-viewer may be distracted when receiving a message because the music next door is loud; a dog is barking; children are running, yelling, or screaming; the listener-viewer is hungry; a phone is ringing; a jet plane is flying low; a timer in the kitchen is ringing; someone is knocking at the back door; the radio or television signal is picking up static; the announcer's voice is annoying; the volume is too high; plus hundreds of other distractions that haunt most listening and viewing environments.

As you think about these stress-producing pressures, you will realize they are always present, and you will begin to understand how essential it is that you, the copywriter, always think of encoding in terms of the listener-viewer's socioeconomic environmental distractions as well as the listener-viewer's personality dominances. The listener-viewer's response will not be the same as yours. That is why coping with the listener-viewer's distractions is important to you. It is your responsibility as a writer to get through to the receiver and create a positive and favorable feedback that expresses itself in words, actions, or both. If no one buys the product, your message is a waste of time and money.

Finally, a writer's encoding must help each receiver enjoy hearing the message in spite of all the personal and environmental distractions that may be present. When the listener-viewer enjoys a message, a positive feedback is more likely to occur. Keep these problem-causing factors in mind as we examine the several steps that interrelate broadcast communication as process.

Broadcast Communicating as Process

Encoding The first step by a source in encoding a message for broadcasting involves more preparation than is realized by most beginning writers. For example, the preparation of an advertising mesage for broadcasting in any large city usually involves many people and several business organizations. The commercial, let us say, is to be prepared by an advertising agency. Assume that the commercial is for a new product.

First, the facts that are to be used by a writer in encoding a message about the product must be made available to the agency. The purpose of a commercial message is to supply information about a product to the receivers, the listener-viewers. Therefore, the need for facts about the new product requires consultation with the manufacturer or his representatives. These representatives may include the manufacturer's lawyers, plus many other authorities in the company. The agency responsible for preparing the commercial message must also be sure that all the facts it receives about the product are correct. Naturally, the agency's representatives and lawyers will most likely contribute to the pool of information.

If a conference is held, a detailed discussion takes place by all involved. Certain ground rules are established about what can and cannot be written about the new product. Much of what is acceptable is determined by the laws governing broadcasting and the rules and regulations concerning similar products. Naturally, most of what must be considered is common sense as it relates to the *communication process*, although enthusiasm for a product has a way of making sense uncommon.

A positive feedback response from the thousands of listener-viewers who receive the message is the purpose of all advertising. Advertising messages are prepared and produced to help people make decisions about a product in terms of their needs. Advertising is not written and produced at great expense to please the whim of the advertiser, the writer, or the broadcast service, regardless of how the content and intent of some messages may sound.

After the various members of the source have agreed upon the information to be used in the commercial, the agency writer, or writers, encode a message. Then the agency's lawyers check what has been written to determine whether the message implies something different from what it is supposed to imply. There must be no legal slip-up, there must be no statement that can be interpreted as being false or misleading, and certainly there must be no unintentional double meanings.

After the legal checking is complete and the message has been rewritten (if necessary), the copy is then reviewed by the advertiser. The advertiser's lawyers may also be called in to check the copy. This checking is done from the company's frame of reference. This checking and rechecking the message goes on until all parties are satisfied with every detail of the message's content in relation to receiver decoding and anticipated feedback response.

Whether you write for a large agency or a small one, preventive error procedures similiar to those described here are essential during the encoding process if your message is to be totally acceptable for airing and decoding.

In many small stations there may be no lawyer to help check the legal aspects of what is written. Nonetheless, the need to adhere to facts and see that they are within the bounds of the law and good taste exists for all writers of radio and television messages.

Message Thus far in our discussion we have been concerned with basic procedures that involve the *encoding* of a message. Let us assume that all those involved have agreed what is to be included in the message and that it has been written and approved. But the final draft of the message, the way it will appear on the air, will be determined by how it actually sounds, or how it sounds and looks, after it has been produced.

Therefore, the final step in preparing the message for *receiving* and *decoding* is producing and recording it on audiotape for radio and on videotape for television. During this procedure the writer should be constantly aware that if the commercial is for radio, then the announcer, the actors, or both may influence the meaning through oral interpretation. If the commercial is for television, then the oral interpretation as well as the visual may determine whether the message is acceptable and ready to be turned over to the broadcast service for channeling.

What all these routines add up to is that writing for radio or television is not a simple matter of having some information and turning the writer's imagination loose to do the job. Of course imagination and creativity are essential. But whether you work for a small station or a large agency, the encoding procedure of a commercial message is the result of compromise by all those involved in the source. Compromise is especially important to the writer. Compromise may also influence production because the message and the media must work together.

Every beginning writer should practice visualizing the message in terms of its completed form. That is, the writer must think of the message in terms of the audio, what the announcer says, or in terms of what the characters imply in their dialogue. Some writers think of the message in terms of the visual—how sight sensations interpret the action, the movement, and how the color blends or contrasts on the television screen. But before the writer reaches that stage in message development, he or she will discover it is the person paying the bills, including the writer's salary, who has a lot (and sometimes the most) to say about what can and will be said in the completed message.

The following incident indicates that there is always a specific need to check and double check a message before it is broadcast. A double-entendre statement by an ad writer provoked a $100,000 lawsuit. It was filed against the station's manager and owner, even though a correction was made immediately. The suit was settled out of court, but the owner-manager from that time on began prerecording and double checking every commercial that went on the air. Many stations today prerecord commercials to avoid this problem.

Channel   The writer for radio and television does not have much control over the process that gets a radio or television message to the receiver. The control the writer exercises depends on, and is determined by, the size of the station, its location, and its dependence on network affiliation. This is true whether the station is radio or television. In some stations the writer is responsible for getting the copy into the continuity book. At other stations the writer is responsible for getting the message recorded and the cartridge (cart), or whatever other device may be in use, in its proper place.

In some stations the writer with vocal talent may voice some of the messages. In other stations the writer's responsibility ends when production is furnished with a copy of the message and an appropriate cue sheet. From that time on, and until the message reaches its intended receivers, there is little the writer can do, or does do, to assure proper channeling. The engineers and the technicians take over that responsibility.

What all this means is that the writer is not responsible when there is a disruption in the power circuit and the station's signal suddenly leaves the air. Neither is the writer responsible when the channeled audio becomes garbled and the color fades. Nor is the writer responsible for the increase or decrease in the intensity of the audio signal when the message comes on.

How the channeling contributes to the effectiveness of the message is determined by the efficiency of that miracle known as radio and television electronics, both sending and receiving, and by those individuals who are responsible for getting the message to the many receivers in the coverage area.

Receiver   The true receiver of every broadcast commercial message is the listener-viewer in the coverage area. And because the listener-viewer is important to the financial well-being of the station, the writer must take into consideration not only the demographics concerning the receiver but many other aspects of the listener-viewer's personality.

Decoding   Understanding how environment influences *decoding* is a must for the copywriter. For example, a 7:00 A.M. to 8:00 A.M. automobile commuter is socially and economically a different decoder from the 8:00 A.M. to 9:00 A.M. commuter. The same may be said of the various periods of home-bound traffic.

Much has been written by specialists about the preferences, fears, prejudices, and need to cope with stressful situations by those who use their car radios on the way to work and on their way home. Certainly many stations recognize the car driver's need to cope with the problem of getting to work on time. Consequently, in many metropolitan areas it is possible to tune to certain stations and be told by a voice from a helicopter all about the traffic between the commuter and his or her job. Also, all aspects of the weather are of great concern to the urbanite commuter who needs to punch the clock at a given time or hopes to get home safely.

Therefore, as a copywriter whose responsibility it is to get a message to individuals, you need to study the surveys and the research about people in your coverage area. And you need to consider more than just the listener-viewer's interest in sex and hunger.

Studies of, and attention to, human needs will help your writing influence the nature and direction of the decoding to your messages. It is imperative that the receivers, wherever they may be at the time, feel and believe that your message is not imposing on their privacy or personal rights to the airwaves. The stations with messages that contribute to problem solving, whatever the nature or the need, are the ones with the greatest number of receivers with positive feedback.

Feedback   A few years ago, a load of peaches received inadequate refrigeration before reaching its destination in a large city. As a result of this oversight, the peaches were ripe and ready for canning when the transporter arrived. The manager of the large store knew that most of the peaches would spoil if the usual routine, putting the fruit in cold storage and handing it out as needed, was followed. Instead, he called two radio stations and ordered commercials that offered peaches ripe for canning. The price was by the box and at a cost much below the market rate. Within three hours after the first message went out to the receivers, every box of ripe peaches was sold. In terms of communication as a process, the advertiser received positive feedback to his message.

As previously noted, the broadcast copywriter must constantly keep in mind that all feedback is intended for the advertiser, not the station, except when it too offers a product for sale.

When unsolicited feedback comes directly to a station, that feedback is usually a complaint. Such complaints take on many forms. For example, a 10,000-watt radio station located in a rural area with a large university carried three ads daily for a local jewelry store. The ads were prepared by a writer at the station, read over the telephone to the jeweler, and okayed by him. Nevertheless, the jeweler fancied himself a communication expert to the extent that not a day went by that he did not call about something following the announcer's interpretation of the copy. As a matter of station policy the assistant manager always sat by the phone for one minute after each message was aired to take the jeweler's call personally. To do so was good public relations with this account.

However, not once in ten years did the jeweler call to congratulate an announcer, or the writer. And while the jeweler suggested interpretation changes, he did not insist that they be made. And not once did the jeweler ever hint about canceling his contract. He did not cancel because statistically there was a high correlation between each ad and the specific number of sales: positive *feedback*. Investment in the commercial time was good business for the jeweler.

In general, the larger a station, the more difficult it is for a copywriter to receive specific feedback about his or her copy outside the station. While receivers may call to complain about performance or the signal level, they are less likely to call about message construction and offer suggestions that will be of specific help to the writer.

The broadcast copywriter who is serious about the work should remember that positive feedback is considered to exist when the listener-viewers respond to the commercial by showing up at the place of business and buying the product. Other indications of positive feedback are evident when the listener-viewer prefers tuning to your station to hear your commercials, when the manager calls you in and gives you a raise, or when you receive an offer from another station to write for it at a higher salary.

SUMMARY

Keep in mind that understanding the various steps in the communication process is important to a copywriter's success. Wherever you work as a writer, before a message can be written, you need to explore fully the problems involved in encoding and in obtaining appropriate feedback to your message. Once the message is prepared, it can be turned over to the proper authorities, whose responsibility it is to see that it is adequately channeled. By the time the message reaches the receiver, it is too late for the writer to have second thoughts about improving it.

Finally, every copywriter must remember that communicating is a continuing process that takes place under varying conditions. The writer must accept the fact that there is no terminal focus. In other words, there is no one way of doing a job right every time. For not only is writing copy a continuous process, it is also a dynamic one. Every writer should take what he or she can from every communication experience and employ it, if it is applicable, to the next copywriting effort.

Writing standards are determined by human standards. That is why the changes that occur in radio and television copywriting, plus the need to make adjustments to those changes, make working in the broadcast industry an exciting adventure.

CHAPTER 2

Language
and
Copywriting

In today's commercial world, special knowledge plus adequate preparation help human beings perform competently and capably. For example, special knowledge and adequate preparation made it possible to lift two space-ships from their pads at Cape Canaveral, place them in orbit, and when the missions were complete, fly them back to earth.

The chapters that follow contain special knowledge that will help you acquire and develop skills essential to becoming a commercial copywriter.

THE SOCIAL NEED FOR COMMERCIAL MESSAGES

There is no evidence that prehistoric people gibbered to their neighbors about new food sources or about stones that made better spear points or axe blades. There is historical evidence that they communicated about how to fulfill physical needs for food. They communicated this information by placing visual images, carvings and paintings, on the walls of the caves in which they lived.

In the United States before the development of the telegraph, the Plains Indians used smoke signals to communicate messages. The early

American Indian and settler developed ways of exchanging commercial information with their hands and bodies. These procedures were called sign language. In fact, from the time of the town crier, communication has helped individuals acquire goods and services.

What will come next to speed up our ability to communicate to large numbers of people simultaneously is not known. We do know that until technical advancements are made beyond our current imagination, radio and television commercials will continue to be in great demand.

We know too that the writing of commercials will continue to be a broadcast priority, both locally and via satelite, because advertising on radio and television is the most expeditious means by which attention can be directed to the availability of a product or service.

While we may object to the "incessant din of commercials" during a favorite program, we know that the level of our economy could not exist if our communication systems were not supported by advertising. Neither would the communication of news nor the abundance of entertainment on radio and television be available on a minute-by-minute basis if it were not for the fact that broadcasting communicates commercials about products and services.

A BASIC PROBLEM IN COMMERCIAL COMMUNICATION

A basic problem in communicating about products and services frustrates most copywriters. When an advertisement is presented on radio or television, it is in effect asking the listener-viewer to change his or her lifestyle to accommodate the product or service. Because a lifestyle is a series of habits with which the individual feels most comfortable, change is generally resisted. For example, a lifestyle may be as individually self-satisfying as that of Mr. Anonymous when he said:

> *I eat my peas with honey.*
> *I've done it all my life.*
> *It makes the peas taste funny,*
> *But they sure stick on my knife.*

Most listener-viewers have aspects of their lifestyle that they do not want to give up. No doubt you have personally experienced negative feelings about requests to change your way of life. If you have felt negative about such requests, perhaps the request was not adequately communicated. It takes a special understanding of words and a special skill to turn words into language that is capable of convincing listener-viewers.

Writing a commercial is not as simple as it would seem. Most of us know only the "scatter-gun" procedure. That is a method advocated by a certain duck hunter who said, "I don't take aim at just one duck! I fill the air full of shot and let the birds fly into it."

To avoid this simplistic technique, let us explore how meanings exist in human beings and may be selected and placed in language to change attitudes that are as persistent as those of Mr. Anonymous.

HOW EXPERIENCE RELATES TO MEANING IN LANGUAGE

Psychologists demonstrate through research that our personality is largely the product of our experiences.[1] Research also demonstrates that personality dominances guide us in developing verbal meanings that are characteristic of our reaction to our environment.[2] Psychologists also show that we react to the influences in our environment very early in life.[3] For example, a child instinctively cries when it is hungry. As children we instinctively cried when we were in pain. These cries got us attention. Before long, we were able to differentiate between our mother's response to our cries, and depending on our feelings about our need, we began using a specific cry to get the kind of attention we wanted.

Even as infants, when we felt the need to be satisfied in a hurry, we learned to increase the cry to a yell. Later, if these prelingual sounds did not get us the response we wanted, we tried nonverbal communication. Most of us, even before we learned to talk, discovered we could get attention quickly by banging our head on the playpen floor. Eventually we became mentally and emotionally aware that using a sound that stood for something was a more acceptable way of expressing a desire. It is through the technique of shaping and controlling sound symbols in language that we discovered how to create meanings that would elicit the specific response desired.

While we were children, learning the significance of a sound that elicited a specific response was slow at first. In time, however, we discovered that the original sounds we associated with, say, *bath*, took on a new meaning. Bath was no longer a time for fun. We discovered we could no longer flail our hands and splash water far and wide. Through verbal sounds made by our mother, bath began to mean that we had our hands confined while they were scrubbed, our eyes blinded with soap, and our mother's fingers, wrapped in a thick cloth, shoved and twisted into each

1. J. Dollard and Neil E. Miller, *Personality and Psychotherapy: Analysis in Terms of Learning, Thinking and Culture* (New York: McGraw-Hill, 1950).
2. S. Lazarus, *Psychological Stress and the Coping Process* (New York: McGraw-Hill, 1966).
3. D. O. Hebb, *The Organization of Behavior*, 3d ed. (New York: Wiley, 1955).

ear. What we now experienced in terms of our ability to classify, interpret, and evaluate was that bath was an unpleasant, confining routine. The freedom and excitement associated with the original verbal sound for bath was gone.

The meaning we applied to the experience of taking a bath when we were children is like thousands of other experiences that we constantly select, classify, interpret, store, reevaluate, and use daily in our communicating process. Moreover, these stored response-meanings, regardless of their relation to an external reality, will be used in the future to describe and express new meanings and new concepts. As our experiences change, so will the word choice with which we express meanings and reactions to them.

HOW MEANINGS RELATE TO CONCEPTS

Because they are the product of experiences that are personally our own, meanings are within each individual. As a copywriter, the meanings you develop through language in a commercial may not be as objective or real to the person hearing what you write. Instead, your language may express meanings that are relevant only to you.

Not being understood is an ever present possibility. For example, suppose you write a radio commercial. Then the announcer interprets it. Naturally he or she interprets the language in terms of personal experiences. The listener-viewer in turn takes what the announcer says and subjects it to his or her experiences. Now comes the real test. Is the meaning the listener-viewer conceives the meaning you intended?

Suppose the announcer said, "Paint your walls a light tan for beauty's sake." To most listener-viewers, the meaning conceived is based on experiences associated with that color, not the color itself.

Suppose that instead of "a light tan," you had used the words "a landlord's buff." Note that even though the color remains the same, these three words change the concept the listener-viewer has about that color. The words change the meaning because experience tells the listener-viewer that the color is not only a light tan but also a color frequently used by landlords. Therefore the acceptance or rejection of the color will now be determined by the listener-viewer's experience with landlords and rental properties.

Fundamentally, language written for any broadcast commercial can be effective if the writer has the ability to use language that gives the listener-viewer an experience in terms of what he or she already knows. Meanings cannot be transferred from one mind to another, they are the result of calling up experiences that are already familiar to the listener-viewer.

HOW CONCEPTS RELATE TO LANGUAGE

We have a fundamental need to communicate. We do this with written and verbal symbols. Through language that stands for specific aspects of reality, we are able to communicate the sounds and reverberations of mountains, valleys, lakes, rivers, streets, squeaks, grunts, and clanks, and even the complexities of modern civilization. Through the use of agreed-upon meanings, one human being is able to make known to another human being that which is being seen, heard, thought, and felt. In fact, society as it is today could not exist if each individual did not have the ability to convey agreed-upon concepts through language.

HOW LANGUAGE RELATES TO FRAME OF REFERENCE

We develop word and language experiences by becoming aware of objects and things through our senses. We enjoy these experiences or dislike them because they extend or limit our ability to feel, smell, taste, see, and hear. This process is called *perceiving*. Attaching meanings to things and objects because of our specific experiences with them is called *developing a frame of reference*. Your response to each thing you see, feel, smell, taste, and hear indicates your preference. That is why a certain frame of reference has a specific meaning to you but may mean something different to the listener-viewer who hears or sees your commercial. Understanding how you and others relate to a given frame of reference is perhaps the most important factor you can pursue in developing an ability to write copy.

HOW FRAME OF REFERENCE RELATES TO SELF-CONCEPT

Words are the basic communication ingredient used by writers. As such, they are a subset of our most useful communicating device, our frames of reference. If we limit each frame of reference to our individual self-concept, however, we may be limiting the meaning and therefore the function of the messages we write. Such a limitation in meaning often occurs because we allow the dominances of our personality to take over. When our self-concept dictates our choice of words in language, the meaning may be perfectly clear to us, but it may not be clearly understood by others.

For example, what frame of reference (viewpoint, meaning, experience) do you think of, recall, or visualize, when you hear or see the multimeaning word *fire*. Normally the frame of reference is determined by your dominant self-concept because the word alone has no additional words to give it a specific meaning. Therefore, if you are a grammarian, you will think of the word fire as being either a verb or a noun. From the point of view of grammar, you know that as a verb, the word fire represents an action; as a noun, it represents something that is burning.

But the word fire, even though it is the only clue, has the potential for calling up experiences found in other frames of references. Suppose you no longer enjoy the privilege of working at a specific job. The reason you are not working there is that the person in charge added one word to "fire" and said, "Fire him!"

The experience of being fired from a job gives you a frame of reference that may be upsetting to you, and as a result it may shake your self-concept every time you hear or see the word fire.

If the word fire had a special meaning to you, would you understand what is meant when you read "'Fire that engine!' shouted the captain?" Actually, the captain's use of the word fire in his frame of reference means that the person spoken to is to build a fire in the steam engine of a ship.

If, during a military advance, a sergeant yells, "Fire that house!" would you know what to do? Specifically the command means to set fire to the house so it will burn to the ground.

The meaning indicated by each of the following statements is relatively clear to most of us because the additional words isolate each frame of reference from all other meanings.

THESE ROSES ARE RED AS FIRE.

DON'T BE WITHOUT FIRE INSURANCE.

KEEP THAT FIRE IN YOUR FURNACE, NOT IN YOUR FLUE.

Many times, even when words are well controlled, there may be a problem. Here is a specific example of how meaning may remain outside the self-concept. A psychologist was using hypnosis to help a student suffering from hypertension. One day, while the patient was being treated, the doctor gave her a posthypnotic suggestion. He said, "I want you to go home now and at ten o'clock tonight you will take a shower, go to bed, and fall sound asleep."

After the session, the young woman went back to her room in the dorm and began packing. Her roommate came in and asked what she was doing.

"I'm going home."

"Why?" asked the roommate.

The girl thought and then said, "I guess because that's what the doctor told me to do. Then at ten o'clock tonight I'm to take a hot shower, go to bed, and fall sound asleep."

"You can do that here," insisted the roommate. "Why do you need to go home for that?"

The student thought and then answered, "I guess because that's what the doctor said."

The rommate called the doctor and explained what was happening. He realized immediately that the language with which he had created a frame of reference for home (where you now live) was not the same as the self-concept of home held by the young woman. She was literally doing what she had been told.

Confusions like this imply reasons why you must constantly keep in mind that listener-viewers are moved to respond to a commercial message only when their self-concept is adequately related to the frame of reference with which they are asked to identify.

WRITING FOR THE SELF-CONCEPT OF OTHERS

As a beginning writer, you normally use your concept when turning ideas into a message. This dependence on your own concepts is normal because your background experience is not as detailed as it eventually will be. But you can avoid letting your concepts limit your meanings by using words called *fact classifiers*. Fact classifiers will help you expand the listener-viewer's frame of reference in a commercial. For example, suppose you heard the statement:

ALL TAXPAYERS REPORT TO THE TAX OFFICE JUNE 16.

An objective analysis of that statement indicates that it is referring to persons who pay taxes. Nevertheless, considerable confusion may arise because the meaning of the message depends upon the word *all*. Does the message literally mean *all taxpayers* must report to the tax office? If the state levies a tax on purchases, then everyone in the state must report. Perhaps the statement means that all property taxpayers are to report? Or does it mean that taxpayers who own cars are to report?

Obviously, certain words must be added to classify and qualify the statement if the message is to be understood.

To help solve such language problems, remember that a statement is defined as an objective observation capable of being proved. In other words, a statement must be qualified if it is to communicate specifically. In this way, and in this way only, will the statement communicate what is meant.

In addition to words that can be used to specify meanings, there are words that create nonspecific meanings. You learned to use these emotionally connotative words as you were growing up because you sometimes confused them with fact words. You were not then aware that emotionally connotative language has no specific reference. All it can convey is something about the way the person using it feels. For example, suppose when you were twelve years old, you said to a friend, "You're a mean old thing!"

Only the attitude of how you felt about your friend is communicated.

Now suppose your friend said to you: "Hey, you turkey! You make me sick!"

Factually, you are not a turkey. Neither did you make your friend sick. All the language choice in these statements does is indicate an emotional attitude held by the individual making the statement.

To get emotionally connotative language to mean what you want it to mean is not easy. In fact, human beings use hundreds of these expressions daily. They are an easy way to express a feeling. For example, the word *pretty*. That word may be used to help connote a feeling or an attitude. But the kind of feeling or attitude meant is not clear without qualifying it in language.

What do the following phrases really mean: pretty girl, pretty picture, pretty scene, pretty face, pretty steep, pretty dumb, pretty honest, pretty hard, pretty tall, pretty short, pretty good, pretty loud, pretty bright, pretty long, pretty stupid? Surely each meaning of *pretty* does not represent the same feeling, attitude, or concept.

Many words connoting extreme opposites in emotions and feelings have vague meanings unless they are qualified. Examples of some of these combinations are:

honest . . . . dishonest
intelligent . . . . stupid
beautiful . . . . ugly
cowardly . . . . brave

Listen to your peers and you will discover that many words in current usage are vague and relatively meaningless. They represent emotional, not factual, values. They are not values that have a common denominator. Therefore, the meanings suggested by such words are at best generalities. They express an emotional concept rather than the nature of an event.

MEANING AND OTHER-DIRECTEDNESS

One fact about commercial broadcasting is paramount. It is capable of communicating an advertising message to an infinite number of individuals at the same time. Because broadcasting has this capacity, many beginning writers tend to assume that a station's financial success is assured because the commercial message is being transmitted.

The truth is far from this electronic possibility. What determines success in the broadcast business is that each message elicit a positive feedback response from the majority of each station's listener-viewers. If feedback does not occur with considerable regularity, the advertiser will not continue to buy advertising time from the station. And without advertising support, a commercial station cannot continue to broadcast.

One reason that a positive response does not always occur is related to the quality of a commercial station's copywriters. Analyses of commercial writing indicate that a greater number of positive responses occur when the advertisement is written by someone who has a knowledge of human motivation and uses it.

According to leading sociologists and psychologists, human responses can be produced by a certain dominant socioeconomic attitude referred to as *other-directedness*. Response that is other-directed is the result of the listener-viewer's tendency to concentrate on external rather than internal values. In other words, human beings are concerned with how others in the same social milieu appear and behave so that they too can appear and behave similarly.

That people are other-directed is used by leading advertising writers to help gain listener-viewer attention and response. It is a technique used in the communication of information about all forms of goods and services related to femininity or masculinity and to social status. When other-directedness is combined with external inducements, individuals with a desire to possess money, prestige, leisure, rest, physical comfort, and efficiency are likely to respond positively to the message.

As a beginning writer of commercial copy, work to remove the internal inhibitors that delay the listener-viewers' acquisition of a product or service. The following example illustrates how a writer can combine an appeal to other-directedness with external inducements and in so doing gain a positive response.

IF YOU'RE LIKE MOST PEOPLE, YOU ENJOY SITTING DOWN TO A CUP OF
HOT COFFEE OR TEA. ESPECIALLY THE FIRST THING IN THE MORNING.
IT TASTES GREAT AND GIVES YOU A LIFT.

In the opening statement of this commercial there is a linkage between other-directedness and external inducements. This combination helps turn any tendency toward internal inhibitions into an inducement that is taken over by external appeals.

Many times, however, the writer fails to make this linkage clear. Sometimes the writer overapplies the technique and in so doing conveys the concept that ownership or use of a product or service will bring about an immediate change in the individual's lifestyle. Here is an example of language inducements that got away from one writer.

TAKE REDUCEO AND WATCH THE RESULTS IN YOUR MIRROR.

Life would be idyllic indeed if problems of weight, or any problems, could be solved this simply and quickly. The facts are that most human physical change requires a reasonable amount of time before it becomes evident. Weight loss, even with starvation, does not consist of a quick transformation physiologically, neurologically, or psychologically. Change in human beings cannot be accomplished as easily as putting on a pair of shoes or slipping into fancy underwear.

CONTROLLING LANGUAGE THAT CREATES FEAR AND SUSPICION

Exaggerated claims about a product also cause the listener-viewer to stop listening and develop mistrust. Exaggerated claims also remind the listener viewer of *caveat emptor*, let the buyer beware. An example of how exaggeration may create fear and suspicion is apparent in the opening of the following commercial.

BABIES HAVE AN OVERWHELMING PREFERENCE FOR THE CRIB DIAPER SERVICE FOR REASONS OF HEALTH AND COMFORT.

Such a sweeping statement invites the listener-viewer to take exception to what is said about the product. Every mother, whether she has read Dr. Spock or not, knows that a baby does not have an "overwhelming preference" for anything until she helps it grow and discover preferences. She also knows, or soon learns, that while a baby cries for many reasons, a special diaper service is not one of them.

The basic flaw in the language of this commercial is that neither of the self-concepts in the opening of the message "Babies have an overwhelming preference for the Crib diaper service for reasons of health and comfort" is backed by evidence. The statements are not facts but value judgments.

The assertions are obviously made by the writer in the hope that a mother listening will assume a causal relationship between herself, her child, and the product. This kind of cause-to-effect writing tends to jeopardize the integrity of the advertiser, the station, and the writer.

Another example of how word and language choices may create fear and suspicion is found in the following:

MOTHERS! I WANT TO TALK TO YOU ABOUT YOUR CHILDREN!

Such an admonition not only arouses suspicion but creates defensiveness. No matter what is said thereafter, the mother will continue feeling defensive about what the announcer implies he knows about her child that she does not.

In general, commercials that begin with sweeping generalities so that attention may be gained are likely to create negative feelings about the product or service.

AVOIDING LANGUAGE THAT CREATES NEGATIVE REACTIONS

Every writer sooner or later discovers that many words used in face-to-face communicating cannot be used in messages over the air. When such words are used, they are likely to create high-and-mighty-sounding attitudes. The primary troublemakers are the personal pronouns: *I, you, me, my, mine.*

Use of these words often creates a feeling of "big I and little you." When this occurs, the listener-viewer feels that the advertiser's ego is showing. Use of these words also creates a feeling of being talked down to, instead of being talked with.

To better understand listener-viewer response to the use of the personal pronoun, we asked listener-viewers for their reactions to the following statements. Here is a consensus of what they said:

I DON'T KNOW ABOUT ALL OF YOU, BUT I BANK WHERE THE IMPORTANT PEOPLE BANK.
"This is blatantly snobbish and turns me away from that bank."

I'LL USE MICHEM WHETHER YOU DO OR NOT.
"So what! I still don't have a good reason for using it."

I KNOW COFFEE AND I KNOW WHAT I LIKE.
"Sounds like an ego trip."

I WOULDN'T DO THIS IF I WERE YOU!
"An actor telling me how to take care of my car?"

MY DOG IS GETTING THE NUTRITION HE NEEDS BECAUSE OF DEPOT.
"Implies my dog isn't getting the nutrition he needs if I don't buy Depot. I'm a dummy?"

AT TENTH NATIONAL WE UNDERSTAND YOUR PROBLEMS.
"They're trying to make me feel that no other bank can understand my banking problems. The other banks wouldn't be in business if they didn't."

DON'T EVER CALL THIS A REGULAR BATTERY.
"That actor is trying to intimidate me, and I don't like it! I'll buy other batteries!"

TOO BAD YOUR WASH IS ONLY SECOND RATE.
"This is trying to make all housewives feel guilty. To hell with the product."

ISN'T IT ABOUT TIME YOU OWNED ONE?
"Gives the impression that the customer has been using poor judgment."

AREN'T YOU GLAD YOU USE SPRIG? DON'T YOU WISH EVERYONE DID?
"Gives a superior impression of a soap. Seems snobbish."

SELECTING LANGUAGE THAT SAYS WHAT YOU MEAN

The responsibility of a copywriter is to be accurate. The way to achieve accuracy is through an adequate choice of words. Most words do an even better job when they are given a helper. The following suggestions about verbs and adverbs have been time tested. Their use is known to all top writers.

Verbs are words that can be used to indicate an action. Example: *The man went home.* "Went" is a verb. The man did the action.

Adverbs are words that can be used to describe the nature of an action. Example: *The man went home quickly.* "Quickly" is an adverb explaining the nature of the man's action.

This particular use of a verb and an adverb slows down the action. As a result, clarity and accuracy become cluttered. Therefore, instead of using an adverb, the writer should select a verb that will also indicate the nature of the action being performed. Example: *The man sprinted home.* A different meaning is indicated by the verb *staggered.* The verb *tottered* suggests a third meaning. "Tottered" suggests age or something about the man's physical condition in addition to the nature of his locomotion.

The following list of simple verbs describe human activities.

bear	drop	pull	strike
blow	fall	push	talk
break	get	put	take
bring	give	run	tear
call	go	stand	tie
carry	hang	stay	throw
cast	hold	set	touch
catch	keep	shape	turn
come	lay	show	walk
cut	let	skip	wear
do	look	step	
drive	make	split	
draw	pick	stick	

Abstract ideas may be expressed by combining a *verb* from the above list with an appropriate *adverb* in the list below. Not every verb can be combined with every adverb, but if you explore the possibilities, you will find you can develop a list that will express thousands of abstract ideas.

about	away	out
across	back	over
ahead	down	together
along	forth	through
apart	in	under
around	off	up
aside	on	

To create an abstract idea, take one of the verbs and combine it with each of the adverbs to see how many new ideas you can discover. For example:

come about	come apart	come in
come across	come back	come off
come ahead	come aside	come on
come along	come forth	come over

You will find that any list of adverbs may be combined with any list of verbs to create additional words for additional meanings. Such adverb-verb or verb-adverb combinations are a characteristic of the English language and are constantly being combined to express new ideas and new meanings. For example:

blackout	lineup	toss-up
breakthrough	pinup	touchdown
checkoff	sitdown	tryout
close-up	stand-in	update
home run	strike-out	walk-on

Always select the word or word combination that describes the nature of the action you wish the listener-viewer to understand. As a copywriter, you will discover that all concrete actions can be expressed or implied adequately with verbs or verb-adverb combinations, and you will avoid the adverb that slows the action.

Another writing problem in which many beginning writers become entangled is called *worditis*. To avoid this affliction, say everything in as few words as possible. Wordy messages put off bringing the product and the buyer together, many times forever.

A commercial that has superfluous verbiage can be improved by judicious cutting. Another technique is to turn all negative statements into positive statements. The following are examples:

can't be beat (omit)
and don't forget (change to positive: *and remember*)
never to be repeated bargain (omit)
can't afford to overlook (change to positive: *see...*)
for the reason that (change to *since* or *because*)
in order to get (change to *to get*)
that is to say (omit or rewrite)
in addition (change to besides or also)
won't you try Jonnie Bread today and see for yourself (positive revises
        to *try Jonnie Bread! You'll love it*)
don't delay to take advantage (revise to *take advantage*)
this is WXYZ, Chicago (revise to *WXYZ, Chicago.*)

Another form of worditis is *redundancy*. Some redundance is useful, but an excess will strangle your style and the listener-viewer. The following statements are redundant and should be avoided. Consult an unabridged dictionary and discover why.

advanced reservation	is located in
advanced planning	is presently
each and every	new construction
free pass	old adage
in order to	past experience
is currently	personal friend

Another form of wordiness is the overuse of prefixed words. This overuse accompanies the need to develop a lead-in. In these days when time is money, however, habitual use of wordiness may also mean the writer has too little to say and takes too much time saying it. The cure is brevity. Brevity creates specificity, and specificity is compelling. Avoid a wordy lead-in unless it is needed for clarity. Here are some overworked examples:

and now	well listen
just	well then
now	well, sir
simply	yes, folks
so	you know
that is	you see

CONTROLLING WORDS THAT HAVE SINGLE AND MULTIPLE MEANINGS

Some words are better left in the dictionary. And it is self-evident that words with single meanings are easier to use in a commercial than are words with multiple meanings. Nevertheless, words with multiple meanings must be used from time to time. The problem with using multimeaning words is learning how to limit their meaning. For example, *building* means many things about a construction. Therefore, when the word is used, its meanings must be limited. *Igloo* and *wigwam* each mean just one kind of building.

Neither the listener-viewer nor the writer has the identification problem with single-meaning words that it is possible to have with multimeaning words. Single-meaning words usually designate and identify places and things; therefore they generally need little limiting. Here are a few. There are thousands of others in the dictionary.

avocado	molasses
bicycle	peanut
clarinet	reindeer
forehead	skateboard
grapefruit	sunglasses
lyre	surfboard

Words with more than one meaning must be limited by the use of an appropriate word or words. But even when the meaning is limited, the copywriter should avoid using the same multiple-meaning word more than once in a sentence or paragraph. For example, note how meanings become confused and diffused in the following sentence when the word *call* is used excessively.

JACK'S CALL TO HARRY TOLD HIM TO CALL BERT TO GIVE HIS BROTHER A CALL WHEN HE CALLED HOME.

Consult any unabridged dictionary, and you will find approximately forty different usage definitions for the multimeaning word *call*.

Thousands of words in our language are considered to have multimeanings. To illustrate the problem that the copywriter faces when using multimeaning words, here are a few definitions for *fast*.

A friend is fast when he is loyal.
A watch is fast when it is ahead of time.
A person is fast when he or she can run rapidly.
A racetrack is fast when it is in good running condition.

A fast may be a period of noneating.
A ship is fast when it is tied with its mooring lines.
A person is fast when he is tied down.
A person is fast when he or she moves in immoral company.
Some people like to play fast and loose.
Colors are said to be fast when they do not run.
To be fast by is to be near.
To be fast asleep is to be deep in sleep.
Photographic film is fast when it is sensitive to light.
Bacteria are fast when they are insensitive to antiseptics.

CONTROLLING MULTIMEANING WORDS WITH SYNONYMS

Perhaps the most useful way to control a word with several meanings is to use a synonym. All copywriters constantly struggle with this problem. Most professional writers find it useful to develop a large vocabulary of substitute words, synonyms, for the multimeaning words they use most often.

When you develop a list of synonyms, remember a word is classifiable either as a verb or as a noun. Therefore, meanings will vary in terms of whether the word stands for a person, place, or thing (a noun) or whether the word denotes action (a verb). Note the different meanings in the *verb* and *noun* synonyms listed after each of the following multimeaning words.

beef: complain, cow, bull, steer, meat, grumble, lament
chair: head, rule, lead, seat, place, bench, helm, control
circle: ring, girdle, encompass, clique, band, orbit, friends
dough: money, green, cash, loot, bread, bucks, funds, wealth
flame: sweetheart, blaze, fire, passion, zeal, love, emotion
foul: dirty, stormy, unfair, obscene, bad, ugly, base, vicious
free: liberated, unrestrained, uninhibited, complimentary
hamper: binder, impede, basket, bassinet, container, obstruct
handle: feel, grip, direct, operate, touch, manage, manipulate
high: drunk, luxurious, tainted, lofty, towering, good, foul
left: leave, remaining, residual, abandoned, sinister, alone
match: contest, pit, bout, marriage, similar, equal, retaliate
nag: demand, horse, quarrel, pester, badger, importune
pitcher: jug, ewer, vase, urn, one who throws a baseball
police: bull, cop, copper, fuzz, heat, officer, patrol
pop: snap, crack, burst, explode, break, noise, unexpected
railroad: force, pressure, push, train, method, expedite
ran: dash, manage, scoot, direct, sprint, bolt, flee, hurry

rate: motion, cost, judge, score, evaluate, price, estimation
ring: encircle, girdle, encompass, toll, chime, resound, gang
ruler: president, director, governor, authority, straightedge
ship: vessel, craft, deliver, mail, send, boat, gig, raft
spin: twirl, whirl, rotate, gyrate, reel, journey, exaggerate
spring: leap, bound, release, reveal, disclose, season, source
state: estate, say, case, mood, aver, express, area of a nation
stir: move, budge, incite, provoke, agitate, excite, fuss, jail
squash: smash, flatten, destroy, obliterate, crash, vegetable
tan: cure, sunburn, thrash, beige, color, henna, auburn, spank
tear: rip, tatter, break, dash, teardrop, violence spree
traffic: trade, transportation, deal, movement, truck, commerce

These words, and many others, are available in any unabridged dictionary and in any reputable thesaurus. The problem with leaving them in these books until needed is that it takes too much time to find them when they are needed in a hurry. Sometimes you may have to look in eight or ten different places.

CONTROLLING LANGUAGE TO CREATE HUMOR

Fundamentally, humor is based on attitudes toward reality. Max Eastman in his *Enjoyment of Laughter*[4] points out that humor is associated with two aspects of life that are a form of unpleasantness. One unpleasantness is failing to get what you want. The second unpleasantness is getting what you do not want. Some call this *situational humor.*

An example of situational humor is used by the world-famous silent clown, Emmett Kelley. Kelley is given the unpleasant task of sweeping the circus stage. Reluctantly he begins and finds several circles of light on the stage. He is sure these spots of light cannot be swept up. Finally, because he has to get the job done, he gives one spot a push with his broom, and to his surprise it moves and becomes smaller. After considerable trial-and-error effort, he succeeds in decreasing the size of each pool of light; he sweeps the lights into a small heap and onto his dustpan. Then, triumphantly, he carries them out.

Humor that results from getting what you do not want is the basis of a Bran Chek commercial. The leading character did not get what she wanted, her kind of bran. Then a second unpleasantness occurs, that of getting what she does not want: some Bran Cheks shoved into her mouth. When this happens, she finds they taste better than she anticipated. In fact, she finds eating them to be a pleasure.

4. Max Eastman, *The Enjoyment of Laughter* (New York: Simon and Schuster, 1936).

Sometimes a beginning commercial writer has a natural talent for creating and writing humor. Most beginning writers should avoid humor as a style, however, until their ability to control words in language is developed.

One reason that humor may be difficult to write is that we cannot agree just what it is. What is funny to one person is not funny to another. Historically the word humor has lived through many definitions. From the Latin it means to be *moist*. From the Greek is means to be *wet*. In medieval times the word was used to refer to a person's health and temperament, habitual disposition, or personality.

In recent years the word humor has been used to describe that which is ludicrous or incongruous. *Mad* magazine is reported by some to be an example. Perhaps the lowest form of humor, that which is generally absurd, is the practical joke, the prank. Most authorities are of the opinion that society has lived through the need for the practical joke as a way of releasing social tension.

Humor that is at the opposite end of the scale from the absurd is referred to as *wit*. Wit is considered to be the highest form of humor. Even so, the wit that entertained millions twenty-five years ago is now frequently laughed at, instead of laughed with.

What can be concluded about humor is that it is many facetted. It may be timely, regional, local, national, international. Timely humor is short lived, as is *reductio ad absurdum*, that which is reduced to an absurdity. Many authorities believe the commercial that used *You can call me Ray* belongs to this category. Most humor of this nature is good for one time only. It loses its ability to hold attention when repeated.

Primarily humor is a matter of taste determined by the writer's choice of language. And as everyone knows, there is no way of accounting for taste. It is a matter of personal preference. That is why many humor critics refer to commercials prepared by local businesses as *unfunny*. An example is a furniture dealer sitting on the roof of his building, shouting, "Come see me! I'm filled up to here!"

There is also the car salesman dressed in a freakish costume and shouting loudly as he pounds a sledgehammer against a car or a gas pump. These commercials are a combination of the practical joke and the obvious. Humor authorities contend that the majority of people laugh *at* instead of *with* such attempts to be humorous. When you laugh at something, it is usually a laugh of derision. The situation may be remembered, but the purpose of the message is generally forgotten.

Humor authorities contend that wit produces a good feeling, a chuckle that is sympathetically associated with a product. It is positive and therefore attracts the customer. A wide variety of commercials now use wit productively.

Obvious humor in a commercial tends to be less productive because human beings are reluctant to buy what they consider ridiculous or what they believe is beneath their social status, dignity, or self-esteem.

CONTROLLING LANGUAGE WITH DEMOGRAPHICS

There are many ways that demographics may be used.

1. As indicated previously, a commercial is more likely to be listened to when it is written to appeal to the individual's self-concept. That is why some commercials are more successful at one time of the day than another. For example, if you write about a product used specifically by women between the ages of 18 and 35, you do not broadcast it to male listeners between the ages of 35 and 55. The commercial's message must fit its targeted audience. Of course, one may write a commercial to appeal to the 35- to 55-year-old male in an effort to get him to buy a product for the 18- to 35-year-old female, but that is a different strategy and a different writing problem.

To be able to write for a specific listener-viewer the writer must be well versed in the area's demographics. Knowing the demographics is the only way the writer can address the message to a self-concept at the appropriate time. Demographic data should furnish you with specifics about the various age levels. It should give information about the younger listener-viewers, the middle-aged listener-viewers, those over 45, and those over 65. The data should include informtion about financial status: what percentage are lower-income, average-income, prosperous, or wealthy.

Demographic data should also show the percentage of people who are apartment dwellers, how many are homeowners, and where their homes are located in relation to shopping centers. Other vital statistics will include educational levels and personal and community activities available. You should know what books are read, what churches attended, what movies watched, and what clubs and organizations dominate your listener-viewers' interest. You should also know their listening and viewing preferences.

2. As a copywriter, you should know how familiar these potential costumers are with the product to be advertised and how many in the area are already users. You should also know how many are potential users of the product and how the product's price compares with prices of competitive brands. You also need to know the listener-viewers' reaction to cost consideration.

3. Copywriters must know whether the purchase of such products is seasonal and whether people are given to contemplating before they buy, are bargain hunters, or are impulse buyers. Not only should the writer know the market's potential in terms of each listener-viewer group, but the writer should know the extent to which the product will fulfill a need.

4. The copywriter should be familiar with data involving test sales in the area, and should know whether most users of a tested product were satisfied. Specifically, the writer must be conversant with the special features of a product or service that benefits those who use it.

5. There are facts other than pure demographics that you must know about the listener-viewer. Many of these facts are psychological. For example, the copywriter will find nearly all listener-viewers tend to mentally tune-out commercials that do not catch the attention immediately. Keeping the tune-out from happening is what copywriting is mostly about.

6. The copywriter must also realize that many listener-viewers are skeptical about the validity of many statements made about products and services because they know that every commercial is a selling device. As a result, most listener-viewers react negatively if the copywriter is having difficulty presenting his facts convincingly.

7. The majority of listener-viewers know there is little difference between many products and that most individuals appearing in a commercial are being paid for their services.

8. The beginning copywriter should be aware that listener-viewers find news reports more interesting than commercial copy. However, listener-viewers usually do not respond favorably to commercials filled with reportorial information about a product. They will listen carefully to commercials that border on the news format. Also, they stay tuned to commercials presented as reminders about products.

9. The copywriter should be aware that many listener-viewers endow some brand names with magical properties. As a result, the writer can, when appropriate, incorporate this aspect of human nature into a commercial.

10. Listener-viewers also respond to a product because it can be ranked numerically. They like to think of it as a number-one product. Many times, they rank it according to consumer testing service listings, and keep it there in spite of all selling efforts to replace it with another product or service.

11. Listener-viewers also respond to a product or service in terms of the social function it serves. For example, one product helps housewives, another is used by those who consider themselves gourmet cooks, and still another helps a working mother make her life less wearisome.

12. When a well-known product begins to lose its popularity in the consciousness of the listener-viewer, a writer can help the commercial by using the *improvement* routine. Detergents and certain foods are regularly made "new and improved."

13. Every beginning copywriter should be aware that, psychologically, each individual plays the lead in a lifestyle drama of his or her own daily existence. That is why commercials are developed around situations with

which listener-viewers can identify. These situations produce excellent sales results. Life situations in which a product has a major role help the person remember it longer and as a result associate it with those self-concept situations that are a part of each day's normal living.

14. Research has for some time indicated that because of the difference in the physiological, psychological, sociological, and economic relationships of males and females in society, *each sex sees and hears a commercial differently*. These response differences are currently being used in commercials that involve vigorous and vital situations for one sex or the other. There is even a touch of masculine anticulture in some commercials. What the writing in these commercials seems to indicate is that the *macho* male prefers the illiteracy that says his beer has *less* calories. Commercials for females indicate they prefer the literate statement that a product has *fewer* calories.

15. While research also indicates that most successful commercials rarely appeal to both sexes at the same time, one common denominator can be used to make an appeal to both. That common denominator is the feeling of happiness. When you write a commercial for both sexes, your approach will be more successful if it relates to a sense of enjoyment, a feeling of *joie de vivre*—joy of life and living—happiness.

16. Current usage and writing techniques indicate that status awareness should be taken into consideration. For example, the characters in a commercial must reflect the status of the person for whom the product is intended. When a product or service is for a housewife, the writer should never use a corporate personality, a person in a bar, or a schoolteacher to tell the housewife what to do or not do. Housewives, or homemakers, seem to listen best to someone with similar experiences. Furthermore, the dialogue should never deviate extremely from the norm. For some products, a quality language is applicable because, psychologically, people in general hope to move up the social ladder and like to imitate those whom they hope to become.

17. The dialogue of a specific social status should be represented neither by its lower nor its upper dialect. For example, a mechanic who uses the language of an English Ph.D is not likely to sound convincing. Neither is the mechanic who uses the language of a third-grade dropout. The need is for believability. It has nothing to do with the ability of the mechanic. It may be that each is an excellent mechanic, but on radio or television the listener-viewer is less likely to take advice from a communicator whose language is extremely different.

18. The dialect in which you write a commercial should be one that will not call attention to itself and distract from the message. When an extreme dialect is used, it must be combined with a situation that will create high humor, a situation that can truly be *laughed with*. An example of this kind of writing is found in a Volkswagen commercial in which a

driver is forced to pull over by two highway patrolmen who are driving VW Rabbit. The driver is dumbfounded that they caught him. The dialect used by the two officers is not only extreme, it is identified as being from "this paht uh Noth Kehlina." Because the dialect and the situation are exceptionally humorous, the listener-viewer remembers the product. The commercial is especially memorable when it concludes with the Volkswagen slogan in nondialect speech: *Volkswagen has done it again.*

19. The successful use that can be made by altering fact-of-life situations means that the copywriter must constantly search for interesting ways of presenting commercial products and services. Sometimes the rules of writing must be changed. Top writers have demonstrated again and again that on occasion the rules governing writing can be improved by breaking them. But the excellence found in this special kind of writing is usually achieved by those who have "paid their dues" as writers, not by those who are just getting started.

LANGUAGE THAT MOTIVATES PEOPLE TO BUY

1. Although there are many writing techniques, the one that moves products and services best is self-motivation. This becomes evident when the language used allows freedom of choice, or freedom of action toward the product. Psychological research indicates that people respond positively more often when some degree of decision making is left to them. During World War II, people were willing to buy bonds and assume many physically wearying wartime responsibilities because they felt they were part of the total war effort. That was their choice. But during the Vietnam conflict, exactly the opposite occurred in many parts of the United States. People were negative about the war because they felt the conflict had been forced on them.

Similarly, listener-viewers are more likely to respond positively if they are regarded as individuals, as separate personalities, rather than as links in a chain. For the writer of commercials, this means the listener-viewer should be motivated to feel a sense of personal worth. When self-determination is paramount, the listener-viewer responds more readily to the thesis of a commercial message.

2. The copywriter should avoid motivating some kinds of self-determination responses. For example, avoid giving the listener-viewer a chance to say no. This opportunity often occurs when the first statement in a commercial is a question. When the listener-viewer can say no to that question, he or she is likely to stop listening to the rest of the message. To help you avoid opening with a question, remember the cliché "People are little children grown tall," and that children prefer to say no to all questions that interrupt what they are doing.

3. Copywriting experience indicates that listener-viewers are more likely to respond to a *positive statement*. A positive statement is a form of certainty that creates security. The copywriter should, however, avoid making statements that are exaggerations or extreme demands. For example, the following statements are demands that many listener-viewers resent and therefore resist.

DO IT NOW!

GO TO HARVEY'S!

BUY NOW AND PAY LATER!

ORDER TODAY!

THIS OFFER IS GOOD ONLY WHILE THE SUPPLY LASTS, SO HURRY!

YOU'LL NEVER SEE BARGAINS THIS LOW AGAIN!

Some of these statements are threatening because they exaggerate by oversimplifying. The listener-viewer tends to associate any exaggeration, even though it is said positively, with scare tactics and *caveat emptor*.

4. When you begin writing commercials, be sure to use words that are easily spoken. Also be sure the words used are easily understood. Use *people language*. This does not mean using street language or slang. Use language that takes into consideration the listener-viewer's wants, wishes, desires, feelings, and above all, self-concept. Use language that knows its way around. For example, the following statement has a special meaning to those who wear dentures. It does not matter that it is a question.

DO LOOSE TEETH HURT YOUR MOUTH AND YOUR FEELINGS?

The purpose of a well-written commercial is to make it unnecessary for the listener-viewer to sort out details and evaluate a product or service. The purpose of a message is to present facts that are easily understood.

5. One of the more useful ways of achieving a response from the listener-viewer is to avoid stereotypes and clichés. Instead of using stereotypes, be verbally informative, persuasive, and at the same time interesting to the degree that what you say will be listened to, understood, and believed. Moreover, the writer should conclude with a *logical judgment*. And while on the way to a judgment, be sure to identify the advertiser as often as it is reasonable and logical. For example:

HERE'S ANOTHER FIRST FROM AMANA. A FIRST AND ONLY! AMANA IS
THE FIRST AND ONLY MANUFACTURER OF MICROWAVE OVENS EXEMPT
FROM DISPLAYING THE U.S. GOVERNMENT SAFETY WARNING LABEL.

6. It is also essential to emphasize how the product meets the claims made for it in relation to the listener-viewer's needs. To illustrate how this is accomplished, the previous commercial is continued:

THAT'S BECAUSE AFTER PASSING A SERIES OF VOLUNTARY TORTURE
TESTS, THE AMANA MICROWAVE OVEN DIDN'T JUST MEET FEDERAL
SAFETY STANDARDS: IT EXCEEDED THEM. AND NO OTHER
MANUFACTURER CAN MAKE THAT CLAIM. REMEMBER, IF IT DOESN'T
SAY AMANA, IT'S NOT A RADARANGE.[5]

7. At the same time that facts and the brand name are being presented, an emotional feeling about the product should be created. Note how the opening of the next example develops a number of special feelings about the pleasure of eating.

> . . . CHUNKY OLD FASHIONED BEEF SOUP IS SO CHUNKY YOU'LL BE
> TEMPTED TO EAT IT WITH A FORK. BUT USE A SPOON TO GET EVERY
> DROP.

8. The writer should make it clear where the listener-viewer may go to see and/or purchase a product. That information is a must in every message. Most of the time the name and location is repeated. The commercial may also include the department in which the product is sold and the store hours, unless that fact is well known or there are two or more outlets in the area. Here is an example that illustrates the use of some of these musts.

> . . . AND YOU WILL FIND FIFTEEN HARVEST FRESH, SWEET AND JUICY
> ORANGES ARE A DOLLAR AT ALDERMANS. YOU ALSO GET GREEN
> STAMPS AT ALDERMANS.

9. If the commercial is regional or national, then only the outlet is stressed. If it is a drugstore item, handled, say, by Walgreen, then the writer says *Walgreen*. If it is a drugstore item that is available everywhere, then make that fact known. In other words, the brand name and the place where the product may be purchased should be mentioned as often as possible. Repetition of this kind is an important aspect of communicating.

10. As a writer of commercial copy, always keep in mind that a product should not be extolled in isolation. Tie the brand name to a feeling, a need, a desire that is both human and personal. Here are some examples of this technique:

> WHEN YOU'RE OUT OF SCHLITZ, YOU'RE OUT OF BEER.
> WHEATIES, THE BREAKFAST OF CHAMPIONS.
> ORANGE JUICE ISN'T JUST FOR BREAKFAST ANYMORE.

5. Courtesy Amana Refrigeration, Inc., Fred W. Streicher, National Advertising Manager, Amana, Iowa.

IF YOU'VE GOT THE TIME, WE'VE GOT THE BEER.
THE BEER THAT MADE MILWAUKEE FAMOUS.
VOLKSWAGEN DOES IT, AGAIN.
FOLGERS TASTES AS RICH AS IT LOOKS.
PREPARATION *H* FOR HEMORRHOIDAL ITCH AND PAIN.

11. The ability of a commercial to sell its product must come before all else. This means that if humor is introduced, it should be the kind of humor that will sell the product, not just cleverness for its own sake. You have, no doubt, heard and seen many local commercials that do not live up to this promise. The same is true of dramatic action introduced into a commercial. In fact, all creativity must be used as a functional tool. And the general rule governing the use of a tool is that if it does not serve its purpose, get rid of it and get a tool that does. A concept that distracts from the sale of a product has no place in your copy.

12. The same no-nonsense concept should be kept in mind with regard to the cost of producing a commercial. Many creative concepts cannot be used because they cost too much to produce. As a copywriter you need to have a working knowledge of costs and know how to take advantage of them. Knowledge of what can be produced on a given budget is a must for every copywriter who wants to be in demand.

LANGUAGE AND THE LENGTH OF A COMMERCIAL

Radio The best way to learn about the mechanics of a radio commercial is to record a number of commercials off the air during different times of the day. Next, type a copy of each text. Then replay the commercial and compare what you hear with what you have typed. With the use of a stopwatch and a pencil, analyze it. You will discover that the word count will vary with the mood and the speed of the oral delivery. Males say a few more words per minute than females. You will also learn that as a writer of commercial copy, you must allow time for the announcer to take a breath. Each breath interval also allows the listener to react to what is being said. As you analyze these radio commercials you will discover that most straight commercial announcements fall into the following approximate time and word patterns:

A 10-second commercial uses from 20 to 25 words.
A 20-second commercial uses from 40 to 45 words.
A 30-second commercial uses from 60 to 70 words.
A 60-second commercial uses from 150 to 180 words.

Television A similar analysis of a series of television commercials indicates that certain mechanical routines occur. The first is that the 60-second television commercial is almost extinct. The 30-second commercial is the long one today. You will also note that many 10-second commercials are tagged on to other commercials. In fact, the use of end-to-end commercials is common practice.

Your stopwatch will reveal that 10- and 20-second commercials are in the majority. And because commercials are run back to back, a commercial period may begin with one that is 30-seconds and without a pause or transition go into a 20-second commercial and then into one that is 10-seconds. You will also discover that a 20-second commercial will leap without a pause into a 30-second commercial, which in turn jumps into a 10-second commercial, and that a 30-second commercial may be followed by three 10-second commercials.

Station managers and producers talk about two reasons for this change in the length of the television commercial. One reason is the cost of air time. Another is the cost of production. Local television is not as expensive as network television; nonetheless, costs are high. A commercial during prime time on network was recently reported to cost in excess of $180,000. For special prime-time shows, the cost is even higher. The final production of "M*A*S*H" is reported to have cost $450,000 per half minute. The cost of air time is not only creating shorter ads but is responsible for the many different short ads that are seen and heard during a 30-minute television show.

Another cost that has become astronomical on television is the cost of talent. The 1980 *Guinness Book of World Records* says that James Coburn spoke two simple words for which he received $25,000 per word. The words were *Schlitz, Light*.

Another reason that commercials are being shortened is that most listener-viewers remember information better when they receive it in short units. The ability of the mind to remember the short TV commercial is also applicable to the radio commercial.

LANGUAGE DIFFERENCES IN RADIO AND TELEVISION COMMERCIALS

Currently, radio is the medium that people in general listen to while they are doing something else. Some think of radio as a constant companion. Many people turn on the radio when they insert the car key. Listeners who commute to work by car are important to radio stations. The same is true of people who walk the streets with portables blaring or earphones clamped over their heads.

The radio is also important to people while they eat breakfast, do housework, write letters, and pay bills. The radio follows students about most of the day. It is a companion to many during study efforts. In fact, the radio seems to be with people everywhere, regardless of what is occupying their attention at the moment.

The radio commercial is considered by some to be more difficult than the television commercial because radio writing requires words and language that create images in the listener's mind. The television commercial writer can depend on the camera to help create these pictures.

To be a truly effective communicator, however, the writer of both radio and television commercials must use language that will catch and hold the listener-viewer's attention during the commercial. Catching and holding attention is done by stimulating the senses. The writer's language must draw a picture of the product or service. It is not gimmicking that communicates. It is the use of short, specific words and phrases that create mental pictures the listener-viewer remembers. For example, whether for radio or television, the commercial that says *a great little car* produces a more vivid picture in the listener-viewer's mind than a phrase such as *a small exceptional car*.

Many times, a beginning writer is admonished to write in short sentences. Short sentences are dramatic. But if used to excess, they create monotony.

In general, the beginning copywriter should say what is needed to get the idea across without concern for restricting the length of a sentence. The *processes* described shortly will help you judge sentence structure, rhythm, and thought content.

CHAPTER 3

Motivating the Listener-Viewer

ATTENTION FACTORS

Writing a message, whether for radio or television, places limits on the use that can be made of visible and audible symbols. Radio is a *blind* medium. It limits the communication of a message to that which is heard. Television, although it combines the audio with the visual, limits its message through the camera and microphone. The listener-viewer sees and hears only that which is transmitted.

In addition to these limitations, the listener-viewer's environment is frequently filled with disruptions that further limit radio and television reception. For example, the radio listener may be in a car on a noisy highway, in the stop-and-go traffic of a city, or in other distracting places where full attention is impossible.

The television listener-viewer may be in a noisy bar or at home with members of the family. In the home environment attention is decreased by conflicting interests. In fact, environmental distractions tend to reduce most message reception to half-listening and half-viewing. And yet under these conditions radio and television are each responsible for deciding many key listener-viewer attitudes and social decisions.[1]

1. H. L. Cantril and G. W. Allport, *The Psychology of Radio* (New York: Harper & Row, 1935).

Cantril and Allport were among the first to survey the effect that broadcast audio reception has on people. Since then, many studies have measured listener-viewer response. We now know that the nature and extent of listener-viewer attention is basically involuntary because the listening and viewing are not required. Instead, the listener-viewer feels emotionally compelled to turn on the set and listen to or view the program.

An example of voluntary listening and viewing is that of attending a class. It is voluntary because attending and listening are part of the contractual arrangement you argeed to when you signed up for the course.

Helping people listen and view is a specific responsibility of the copywriter. That is why top writers combine the psychological principles found in voluntary listening and viewing with the psychological principles found in involuntary listening and viewing. In other words, getting the listener-viewer to react both voluntarily and involuntarily is more easily accomplished if the writer incorporates what are known as *human attention factors*.[2]

Human Attention Factors

Change is an essential factor if the listener-viewer's attention is to be kept focused. A basic principle of writing is that a stimulus continues to move in a given direction if the intensity of its direction is varied. That is why the copywriter must alternate the importance of each thought. This alternation of a thought, or event, is done by following a major one with a medium or a minor one, which in turn is followed by one that is major. When this occurs, the listener-viewer's interest is maintained.

When the content of a commercial consists primarily of a series of events that are equal in importance, the total effect is monotony if not dullness. When intensity without change dominates a commercial, the listener-viewer is most likely to go for a drink or to get something to eat. He or she may even hit the *off* button.

When a commercial is arranged in a varied interest sequence of major, minor, medium, major sequence of scene and thought patterns, and is climaxed with a major event or thought that gives it a lift through human excitement, the use of change inevitably creates more purposeful listening and viewing.

It is generally agreed that the television commercial writer has an advantage over the radio commercial writer. It is true that, on television, change in the visual can be used as an attention device. But in the final analysis, what the writer has to say and how it is said is the real center of

2. Bernard Berlson and Gary A. Steiner, *Human Behavior* (New York: Harcourt, Brace and World, 1964). G. Murphy, *An Introduction to Psychology* (New York: Harper & Row, 1951).

attention in any commercial. Listen to a commercial that is presented again and again. When the language fails to catch and hold the listener-viewer's attention, the writer has failed.

Repetition is used by a copywriter to increase the listener-viewer's awareness of what is being communicated. Repetition is especially useful in any content that is heavy with facts. Its use helps comprehension and improves understanding. Naturally, all repetition should vary in length and technique. The writer should not repeat just to be repeating.

The beginning copywriter may not need to use additional repetition when following the six-step and seven-step processes presented in Chapter 5. Repetition is a part of these two processes and is used for the purpose of helping catch and hold the listener-viewer's attention. Repetition may also be used for clarifying a point in the latter part of a commercial. For further information and techniques, see Chapter 7, Rewriting.

Every situation or event used to illustrate a thesis, theme, or central idea in a commercial should be carefully examined to discover how *conflict* may be introduced to include competition between the characters or between a character and a situation. The fundamentals of conflict, two opposing forces, are always present when an individual becomes involved in an event or with another person. Such conflicts are an effective means of catching and holding the attention of the listener-viewer.

For example, various conflicts are the normal accompaniment of every sporting event. Various social conflicts are present in the discussion of every problem, need, feeling, or desire. And because opposition is a normal part of human living, most activities that create conflict can be used to develop an ideational or emotional identification with one side or the other of every problem, need, feeling, or desire. When conflict is not an obvious part of a situation, many imaginative and farsighted copywriters keep in mind that conflict is basic to the success of everything that is written for commercial broadcasting, and so they create conflict.

Suspense is the mental and emotional state of listener-viewer uncertainty about the end result or conclusion of what they are seeing or hearing. Suspense is inextricably linked to conflict. Where there is conflict, suspense inevitably follows. That is why suspense is always used as a storytelling device by the commercial writer.

Suspense is needed to get the listener-viewer involved mentally and emotionally in what the copywriter is illustrating in the commercial. As a result of this involvement the listener-viewer becomes more intent. Always, of course, the listener-viewer should feel that the problem, need, feeling, or desire is best solved as suggested in the commercial.

Once a listener-viewer is hooked by the suspense created by the conflict, additional complications can increase the suspense to the extent that, mentally and emotionally, the listener-viewer will literally hang on to the commercial's every word until the final solution. Aristotle in the fourth century B.C. was the first to note the effectiveness of this aspect of oral-aural communicating with the use and help of suspense.[3]

The Importance of Attention Factors

Individuals frequently argue that they should be permitted to make up their own minds about what they should eat, drink, do, or wear—only they know what is best for them. However, psychological studies show that human beings are not always in total command of their ability to be objective about themselves. People have the capacity to reason, but there is a difference between capacity and achievement. Research demonstrates that emotional bias tends to dominate.[4] As a result, people who are uncertain and do not have the experience to make objective decisions prefer to have suggestions made about choices.

Since Overstreet's study of this human characteristic, other psychological research shows that our emotions, feelings, and desires determine our muscle tension, heart rate, and ability to relax or be irritated, rather than our ability to reason and be objective.[5]

These four attention factors, *change*, *repetition*, *conflict*, and *suspense*, are useful in helping the listener-viewer experience the kind of feelings that give him or her hope for the future. These factors are especially helpful to the writer when subtle humor is added to the copy. Fewer negations occur among listener-viewers when humor is present. Naturally, the addition of humor does not mean humor for humor's sake. Perhaps just having a character in a commercial be pleasant or exuberant about solving a situation is a better way to describe it. In other words, the listener-viewer may not agree with what the character says or does, but will not deny the character his or her right to say, feel, or be, if what is said or done is pleasantly disarming.

While you may not always be able to employ this technique, keep in mind that more mental and emotional attitudes are changed with the help of pleasantness and consideration than through the use of fear, anger, or disrespect. This attitude and procedure, facing adversity with a smile, is often referred to as exercising diplomacy.

Many times, of course, when listener-viewer motivation is urgently needed, the commercial copywriter feels that listener-viewers should be shaken from their complacency. Even so, a logical appeal will not always get the job done as easily or as well as an appeal to the emotions through a

3. S. H. Butcher, *Aristotle's Poetics* (New York: Hill and Wang, 1961).
4. H. A. Overstreet, *The Mature Mind* (New York: Norton, 1949).
5. Meyer Freidman, M.D., and Ray H. Roseman, M.D., *Type A Behavior and Your Heart* (New York: Knopf, 1974).

smile or chuckle. In fact, logical appeals are generally effective only when they are combined with objective pleasantry—subtle, mild humor.

USING BASIC HUMAN DRIVES

The use of logic and humor are effective as an approach to catching human attention and motivating response when the appeal is based on the following human drives:[6]

People are concerned primarily with a need to satisfy their physical wants and desires. To this end, people will go without food, clothing, sleep, and even sex. For example, people will work hard and deprive themselves so that they can eventually enjoy a vacation. Parents endure financial sacrifices so that their children can experience the advantages of an education. Many individuals hold two jobs or moonlight to earn extra money to satisfy a want or desire they feel has been, or is being, denied them. This fundamental human drive is often used by radio and television copywriters to capture the listener-viewer's attention and elicit a response.

People direct their behavior toward mastering and achieving a desired goal. While human beings may feel frustrated at times, they are willing to endure and work hard if they believe the effort will help them succeed. For example, most students are willing to work harder than they have ever worked before when they believe they are acquiring an ability in a certain course to become a number-one competitor in the job market. Ask any highly competitive athlete or honor student about mastering something in an effort to achieve a desired goal. From time to time, most successful commercial writers use this form of motivating to catch and hold listener-viewer interest and attention.

People prefer to act and respond in a manner that brings them approval, respect, and admiration. For example, individuals will carefully, and sometimes painfully, avoid actions and events, social and otherwise, that they feel may cause them to be ignored, derided, or looked down upon. Yet these same individuals may join a group to help prevent the construction of a dam or nuclear power plant; they are willing to accept derision today because tomorrow they believe their actions will be recognized as being a form of rightness for which they will receive applause.

The commercial that points out how the listener-viewer can conserve gas and yet keep that big-car feeling by buying such and such a car is making an appeal to the need to achieve status and thereby avoid being ignored. Not being ignored places these individuals in the category with those who have acquired prominence and attention. An appeal to this human drive is especially useful to the copywriter.

6. Berelson and Steiner, *Human Behavior.*

Some people have a basic need to feel wanted, respected, loved; as a result of this need, they act and react accordingly. These individuals will avoid all behavior that may show them in the wrong light. Many, for example, prefer the company of an in-group rather than have to go it alone. These individuals join groups and organizations. Many become church members to achieve social status. They prefer to respond to the in-thing to do. The need to belong in order to be considered loved or respected is a very useful motivational factor to the commercial copywriter.

People prefer to act in ways that dispel worry and anxiety. Some individuals may refuse to ride in an elevator or travel by plane. Others refuse to walk in the streets or parks after dark. They refuse to do these things because not doing them decreases their feelings of fear, uncertainty, and insecurity.

For example, many students feel deficient in certain abilities. Science and mathematics are examples. As a result, these individuals avoid all such courses when possible. If requirements for graduation permit them to select courses of their choice, they choose courses that give them an advantage over their feelings of inadequacy.

In certain advertisements the listener-viewer is urged to consolidate accumulated debts and let a finance company keep them "debt free." An appeal to freedom from social fear ("ring around the collar") is often used by the commercial copywriter.

People need new experiences or adventures to give them a feeling of zest for enduring life. Punching the timeclock is an existence filled with monotony and boredom for many. This occurs in spite of the fact that the majority of jobs can lead to advancement and security. To be able to endure the Monday through Friday routine, the "thank God it's Friday" and "sure happy it's Thursday" exclaimers tend to plan for, and achieve, release on the weekend. They sail, they drink, they romance, they escape. For them, slogans that say "Would good friends go at it that hard for a beer" and "Weekends were made for ——" have great appeal.

Other commercials tell individuals how to give their all in an effort to experience a "youthful zest for life," if not life itself. This emotional factor, the need for new experiences "to bolster one's sanity" is especially useful to the copywriter.

Because the six basic human drives just discussed are specifically related to behavioral patterns, the copywriter can use them advantageously as attention factors to elicit human response. Nevertheless, they should be used with subtlety and consideration.

Diverse responses are likely to occur when an excess of motivational appeals are used in a message. Using too many appeals is likely to turn the copy into a series of generalizations. As previously explained, a generalization is the result of making the same statement about different facts. For example, contrary to how it looks, tastes, and smells, all orange juices are not alike. Neither is anything else regardless of how it seems to be.

Being objective and specific helps motivational appeals create a frame of reference experience overlap. When overlapping occurs adequately during the communication of a message, the listener-viewer silently talks along with the communicator. Many listener-viewers actually move their lips. In this way they momentarily become the communicator delivering the message and kinesthetically experience an empathic response.

UNDERSTANDING SELF-CONCEPT IN OTHERS

As a writer of commercials for radio and television, you need to use ideas in terms of how the listener-viewer sees himself or herself. Most beginning writers soon discover that the language they put on paper relates to the product primarily in terms of the writer's self-concept, not the self-concept of the listener-viewer. This tendency to impose the writer's language on the listener-viewer is perfectly normal because, as explained previously, self-concept is the controlling force in every individual's personality. To understand why and how your personal choice of language may have one meaning for you and a different meaning to each listener-viewer, study the following explanation of personality in relation to self-concept.

DEFINITION: Personality, to most authorities, is the integrated and dynamic organization of the physical, mental, moral, and social qualities of each individual. These qualities are the natural and acquired impulses, opinions, and beliefs that are manifest in relationships with other people in the give and take of a social environment. As a result, these impulses, opinions, and beliefs become dominant in each individual. Therefore, as dominant characteristics, they constitute that individual's self-concept.[7]

We understand from this explanation just why individuals respond positively to language that enhances their feelings or beliefs about themselves, but tend to respond negatively to language that does not. Moreover, we see that a response, be it positive or negative, will occur if the individual's self-concept is involved.

That is why the writer of a radio or television commercial will most often elicit a stronger positive response when the language enhances feelings about what the listener-viewer believes he or she can do or can be. Specifically, the writer must select language that relates to the product or service in terms of the listener-viewer's self-concept.

There are specific misuses of language in relation to self-concept that a writer should always avoid. One misuse creates mental and emotional images with which the listener-viewer resents being identified. For exam-

7. James Drever, *A Dictionary of Psychology*, rev. ed. (Baltimore: Penguin, 1971).

ple, easygoing individuals never want to be thought of as tense. Efficient individuals never conceive of themselves as careless or inconsistent. Identifying the listener-viewer with a self-concept that is contrary to his or her notion of self-concept will generally cause a negative response to a commercial message.

APPEALING TO THE SELF-CONCEPT IN OTHERS

The successful writer uses language that appeals to the listener-viewer's self-concept, to what the listener-viewer thinks he or she is, or wants to become. For example, a person who visualizes the *self* as carefree prefers to respond positively to language about a product or service that enhances the belief that he or she is lighthearted, amusing, and witty. Also, a responsible mother who wants to remove spots from her child's clothing will always choose a detergent that is efficient and reliable.

The *macho* male concept is used in some car commercials, and the female as a sex symbol is used in some perfume and makeup ads. Their use is not by chance. The language in these commercials is carefully selected because experiential evidence indicates that this language is more often successful in turning-on the listener-viewer and in so doing creates a positive response. Such a response helps move the product.

The copywriter for radio and television can become more objective, and therefore more successful as a writer, by developing and using lists of synonyms and analogous words that will remind the listener-viewer of how he or she likes to feel, think, act, and behave. The writer should also compile lists of antonyms, contrast words, to these synonyms and analogous words. The lists of opposites are an indispensable tool. They help the writer visualize and create the characters needed in developing personality likes and unalikes in television commercials.

Any quality book of synonyms and antonyms will help the writer put a ready-reference list together from which to choose the most useful words. What follows are examples to illustrate the kind of word preference that every serious copywriter needs. The synonym list was prepared for each of the previously discussed self-concept attitudes. Each synonym list is followed by a list of antonyms. The antonyms were not selected to parallel the synonyms. Some of these lists are naturally longer than others because human beings have more diverse feelings about some attitudes than they have about others.

Synonyms for *affectionate*: ardent, compassionate, devoted, emotional, likable, loving, passionate, romantic, sensitive, softhearted, tenderness, warmhearted.
Antonyms for *affectionate*: abhorrent, abominate, aversion, coolness, detestation, frigid, hatred, loathing.

Synonyms for *carefree*: amusing, charming, easygoing, funny, happy, humorous, imaginative, jolly, jovial, likable, lovely, talkative, quick-witted.

Antonyms for *carefree*: annoyed, boredom, depressed, fatiguing, inactive, irked, languidness, lethargic, oppressing, phlegmatic, spiritless, tedium, tiring, vexing.

Synonyms for *dominating*: abrupt, aggressive, assertive, bold, bossy, belligerent, cunning, daring, demanding, forceful, grouchy, influential, opinionated, outspoken, persuasive, pompous, possessive, quarrelsome, rebellious, rigid, sarcastic, scheming, self-seeking, shrewd, stubborn.

Antonyms for *dominating*: abject, acquiescent, compliant, cowering, cringing, fawning, ignoble, mean, resigned, secondary, subservient.

Synonyms for *efficient*: ambitious, businesslike, conscientious, decisive, dependable, determined, diligent, effective, energetic, earnest, hardworking, industrious, methodical, organized, perservering, reliable, responsible, thorough.

Antonyms for *efficient*: careless, diverse, disruptive, incapable, inconsistent, ineffective, inefficient, lazy, nonenergetic, unharmonious, unorganized.

Synonyms for *kind*: accommodating, agreeable, altrustic, charitable, cheerful, congenial, considerate, courteous, earnest, faithful, forgiving, friendly, goodhearted, goodnatured, generous, gracious, helpful, humane, honest, kindhearted, loving, pleasing, sensitive, sincere, thoughtful, trusting, understanding, warmhearted.

Antonyms for *kind*: arrogant, cruel, fierce, grim, harsh, inhuman, merciless, rough, savage, unrelenting.

Synonyms for *refined*: adult, charming, cultured, courteous, dignified, elegant, formal, gracious, luxurious, poised, politeness, self-assured, sophisticated, vivacious, well-mannered.

Antonyms for *refined*: common, indecent, indelicate, offensive, ordinary, overly familiar, pretentious, repulsive, revolting, rude, vile, vulgarity.

Synonyms for *reserved*: bashful, carefree, cautious, complacent, conservative, conventional, dignified, docile, formal, frugal, humble, introverted, meek, modest, obedient, old-fashioned, placid, practical, prudent, refined, restrained, reticent, silent, serious, tactful, quiet, withdrawn.

Antonyms for *reserved*: affable, assertive, blatant, boisterous, bold, clamorous, glamorous, extroverted, glib, impetuous, impulsive, outgoing, outspoken, pushy, talkative, vulgar.

Synonyms for *self-assured*: confident, courageous, decisive, determined, idealistic, independent, optimistic, poised, positive, secure, self-controlled, self-confident, self-reliant, self-sufficient, self-satisfied, strong-minded, tenacious.

Antonyms for *self-assured*: bashful, cautious, diffident, faltering, ineffective, ineffectual, modesty, nonassurance, shyness, timidity, vacillating, wary, wavering.

Synonyms for *sociable*: active, affable, cheerful, congenial, cordial, energetic, friendly, gracious, gregarious, genial, happy, likable, lively, neighborly, outgoing, pleasant.

Antonyms for *sociable*: antisocial, belligerent, hatred, hostile, impassive, lethargic, listless, suspicious, unfriendly, unsocial, withdrawn.

Synonyms for *tense*: anxious, excitable, emotional, grouchy, highstrung, impatient, moody, nervous, pessimistic, short-tempered, superstitious, temperamental.

Antonyms for *tense*: assurance, calm, carefree, composed, confidence, easygoing, good-tempered, relaxed, secure, self-controlled, self-reliant.

Synonyms for *trustworthy*: able, capable, careful, cautious, competent, dependable, diligent, honorable, honest, level-headed, observant, practical, reliable, respectable, realistic, responsible, self-reliant, sensible, sincere.

Antonyms for *trustworthy*: deceitful, disinclined, doubtful, dubious, fickle, mistrustful, nondependable, questionable, skeptical, suspicious, uncertain, unreliable, untrustworthy.

Every copywriter will find it helpful to develop a ready reference list of synonyms and antonyms that fit specific writing needs. Such a list makes it unnecessary to look for a new word each time a substitute is needed. Such a list is also an endless source of new ideas.

The list should be developed to support the copywriter's style, thought process, and specialization. The specific purpose for such a list is to help the writer avoid being verbally repetitious and therefore a less interesting writer.

Professionally your synonym-antonym list will help you discover new ways of expressing self-concepts that stimulate the minds of the listener-viewer. Naturally, the broader the reference list, the more self-concepts it will relate to. Understanding your listener-viewers' self-concepts will help you incorporate the attention factors, as well as the basic human drives, into the commercials you write.

CHAPTER 4

Planning the Commercial

TIME AS A FACTOR

Every activity that occupies human effort seems to have procedures that influence the amount of *time* available for performing the task. Certainly this is true of a broadcast commercial. The total air time available determines the number of words that can be used in communicating the message.

Nevertheless, time cannot be considered the only factor that determines the number of words used. The *tempo* at which a commercial is presented also influences the time and the number of words used. *Mood* is another important aspect of time. Another factor is *variation* and *variety* in the inflection of the performer's voice. Females, because they normally use greater vocal variation and inflection than males do, communicate fewer words per minute.

When the writer uses more than one voice to create a talking and listening situation, that combination takes more time and therefore fewer words. Another factor is that no two individuals in a commercial should ever speak at the same rate. Contrasts in vocal rate create variety, which creates interest and helps hold listener viewer attention. Telephone numbers used should be repeated. This repetition requires as much time as needed to speak twenty-five ordinary words.

The kind of commercial, regardless of the total time on the air, is an additional consideration. Most straight commercials may be communicated understandably at a tempo of 160 to 170 words per minute. However, most announcers and professional performers are more comfortable speaking at a slightly slower rate.

Here are nine kinds of commercials related to time and the number of words that may or may not be used in writing them.

The Straight Commercial

The *straight commercial* has long been considered the workhorse of radio broadcasting. A few visuals are sometimes combined with the message, and it is then used to do the same job for television. In fact, many straight television commercials are presented on radio by the audio. The reason for this dual use is obvious. It costs less to write and produce a commercial for two media at one time. And the cost of writing and producing a commercial is an important consideration in the life of all cost-conscious advertisers.

A straight commercial may be thought of as the equivalent of hard news. The similarity is comparable in both content and the style in which it is communicated. A hard-news story consists of basic facts communicated by a newscaster. On radio a straight commercial is generally read in a direct manner without the accompaniment of music or sound effects. It may be presented live or may be on tape. In many radio stations this presentation is the responsibility of the disc jockey on duty. However, because human beings make verbal errors (e.g., "to keep fit and filthy— uh—healthy") plus the tendency to sound the same during each comercial (and therefore monotonous), many radio stations use a different voice for each commercial. Variety is a basic factor in creating interest in a communicated message.

Some stations tape all their commercials to avoid vocal errors. Former students who were especially gifted as straight copy communicators were able to pay their college fees with the money they made taping commercials.

There are a few verbal styles of delivery other than personality that the writer should take into consideration. These vocal styles are used to help vary the sound and sense of straight copy. The announcer may use a friendly conversational style. This style is similar to that of a salesclerk in your favorite store. To create this style the writer develops straight copy that helps the announcer sound friendly.

On occasion the writer must help the announcer be casual and seem to be ad-libbing, as speaking to an intimate or close friend. This kind of communicating is frequently referred to as *soft sell*. As a writing technique it is a crossover into the *personality commercial* (see below). Soft sell uses a slower tempo and requires fewer words.

Regardless of the style of delivery used by the announcer, evidence indicates that, basically, the quality of the writing is responsible for each commercial's success. Quality writing helps assure the listener's reaction to, and belief in, what is being said.

This same coordination between writing and delivery is essential to television communication. In television the talent may get some assistance from visuals and music. But regardless of what is included in the production process, the basic concept of holism is important to a commercial's success. The total effect of a commercial must be greater than the sum of its parts.

Here is a *straight commercial* heard both on radio and television.

MANY TIMES WE FEEL LIKE FLUSHING OURSELVES DOWN THE DRAIN
BECAUSE OF OUR EXCESS WEIGHT. BUT NOW THERE IS REDUSO, THE
TABLET THAT WILL HELP FLUSH UNWANTED FAT AND FLUIDS FROM
YOUR BODY. TAKE REDUSO AND WATCH THE RESULTS IN YOUR
MIRROR. YOU'LL FEEL GOOD ABOUT YOURSELF AS YOU BECOME THE
SIZE AND WEIGHT YOU WANT TO BE. REDUSO IS THE BEST WEIGHT
LOSING TABLET ON THE MARKET.

The Personality Commercial

After the writer becomes familiar with the techniques of writing straight copy, writing the various styles used with the *personality commercial* will not be difficult. These styles are used by both male and female voices on radio and television. Personality delivery, if it is to be a success, requires writing that specifically fits the mood and style (the personality) of the person doing the delivery.

Many radio station announcers become personalities because they communicate their copy in the style and manner of the station's format. This is true whether the format is Top-40 or classical FM. Smaller radio stations seem to use straight copy for this purpose and expect the DJ to do an efficient job of interpreting the message as a personality. However, a must for every writer is to know how the copy is to be delivered and write accordingly. For example, the personality announcer may rhythmically and melodically punch, or emphasize, each word in the copy. With this exaggeration he gives the copy a rhythmic emphasis similar to that of a rapidly beaten drum. This type of emphasis has for years been referred to as *hard-sell* delivery.

The varying degrees of this emphasis are determined by the subject matter. But as every writer discovers, certain words and phrase combinations have to be avoided in writing hard-sell copy. These combinations, when used, exaggerate the rhythm and in so doing call attention to the manner of the delivery instead of the meaning in the message.

To avoid turning out ineffective-sounding hard-sell copy, the writer should avoid using, insofar as is possible, all words ending in *ly*—adverbs. Also avoid using words that have popping sounds, such as *P*, *B*, *D*, and the hissing sounds *S*, *SH*, *Z*. Please note the excessive use of popping and hissing sounds in the following hard-sell copy.

EVERY COLD SUFFERER SHOULD REMEMBER THIS NAME! HILL'S COLD
TABLETS! FOR HILL'S COLD TABLETS ARE ESPECIALLY COMPOUNDED
TO GET AFTER THOSE ACHES AND PAINS, THAT DRY FEVERISH FLUSH,
SOME OF THE MANY THINGS THAT MAKE YOU MISERABLE WHEN YOU
HAVE A COLD! TAKE ONLY AS DIRECTED! GET AMAZINGLY FAST
RELIEF FROM THOSE TORMENTING COLD SYMPTOMS. HILL'S!
H-I-L-L-S! HILL'S COLD TABLETS!

Another frequent misdirected contribution to the writing of hard-sell copy is the creation of the wrong mood for the listener-viewer. For example, most individuals who have a nagging cold do not enjoy being shouted at. They would like to receive a little sympathy. From the point of view of the announcer, hard-sell copy is difficult to read any other way. Be sure the writing style is appropriate for the product.

When writing commercials for a personality announcer, be sure to obtain firsthand information about that individual. For example, is the announcer a star, or a celebrity to the listener-viewers? The writer also needs to know what kind of mood the person's voice communicates. Naturally, your copy must supplement and reinforce the voice.

Finally, hard-sell copy in both style and melody is firm, fast paced, and repetitive.

Another variant used by the personality salesperson is *soft sell.* It too is a technique of delivery used both on radio and television. To comply with these uses the writer must thoroughly understand why the product is to be offered to the listener-viewer in this delivery style. The nature of soft-sell copy implies that it will be presented in a person-to-person, close-up, intimate manner. The copy must imply friendliness and confidentiality.

On radio the personality DJ may improvise the copy in an effort to personalize and create confidentiality and a friendly, intimate vocal relationship with the listener-viewer. On television the soft-sell is used primarily with personal products or where the suggestion of sexual interest is indicated or implied. Soft-sell copy is used with perfumes, colognes, and other products in which the attractiveness of odor may play an important role. In these ads on television the visual is used extensively to reinforce the audio.

Regardless of the style of delivery, when the television personality is well known, he or she is generally placed in full view of the camera. In fact, the personality may serve as a prominent part of the picture. The personality salesperson also makes contact with the product. The automobile and watch industries, and the grocery chains, are especially known for using this commercial format.

When the personality salesperson is less well known, particularly on local television, he or she may not be seen more than once or twice in each commercial, if at all. The amount of time spent showing the person with the product is determined by how well known and how well liked that person is by local viewers. The more the viewers enjoy seeing the personality deliver the message, the more the personality will be seen and associated with the product.

The Multivoiced Commercial

The pure *multivoiced commercial* does not use dialogue technique per se. Neither are questions that require answers an essential part of this style of commercial writing. Instead, one voice may speak the first phrase of a sentence, and a second voice may speak the second phrase, which in turn is followed by the first, or even a third, voice. Sometimes Voice 1 may speak a complete sentence, and Voice 2 then speaks the next sentence.

Fundamentally, a multivoiced commercial is a production device for creating attention. The multivoiced commercial is used most often on radio stations that also use hard-sell technique. Even though multivoice is a production device, it can in no way be considered conversation. Conversation is an aspect of dialogue and is a logical part of the dramatic commercial (see Chapter 6).

The following is an example of multivoiced writing.

1ST VOICE

THE WEEKEND AHEAD CALLS FOR REFRESHING BEVERAGES!

2D VOICE

IF BEER IS YOUR FAVORITE REFRESHMENT

1ST VOICE: CALL YOUR NEIGHBORHOOD DISTRIBUTOR TODAY
2D VOICE: FOR A CASE OR TWO OF MOUNTAIN TOP PREMIUM BEER!
1ST VOICE: THE BEER THAT'S BETTER BECAUSE ITS BREWED WITH
PURE MOUNTAIN SPRING WATER!

2D VOICE: MOUNTAIN TOP PREMIUM BEER HAS BECOME A SYMBOL OF
DISTINCTION AMONG BEER DRINKERS
1ST VOICE: WHO APPRECIATE GENUINE BEER QUALITY.
2D VOICE: THAT'S WHY MOUNTAIN TOP IS THE LARGEST SELLING
PREMIUM BEER IN THE ROCKIES!
1ST VOICE: ASK YOUR DISTRIBUTOR FOR A CASE OF MOUNTAIN TOP,
TODAY!

The Dialogue Commercial

Two voices are, of course, also essential to the *dialogue commercial.*
Dialogue is the result of one source talking to, or asking questions of, a
second source. For example, a dialogue may take place between a source
and a computer, or between a cartoon character and another source. A
vocal source may talk to a member of the animal world. These voice
exchanges can be considered a form of conversation only when the reply is
appropriate for the occasion.

Dialogue is easily written. One source asks a question of, or makes a
statement to, a second source, who answers the question or replies in some
way. This reply may be fulfilled by reading information printed on the
package of a product. In this way an exchange of information takes place.

Or, in a scene, an individual may talk to a salesman in a store. The
person asks a question, and the salesman supplies the answer. One widely
used dialogue situation for this commercial technique is to have a person
talk to a knowledgeable repairman or serviceman. The repairman may be
an electrician, washing machine specialist, plumber, mechanic, or whatever. Generally the individual answering the questions explains why the
object or equipment works well, why it lasts a long time, why it is easy to
maintain, or why it rarely needs repairs.

A dialogue situation exists when two salespersons are talking about a
product or how certain equipment operates. Another form of dialogue is to
have a professional salesperson talk with a novice, or to have a novice
telephone someone qualified and discuss a product or problem in detail. The latter person may be the manufacturer, the dealer, or a service
person.

Hundreds of such situations are available to the imaginative writer.
Fundamentally, the first person in the dialogue is inquiring, and the second
person supplies the needed information. Whatever scene you use, avoid
unbelievable situations. They are generally laughed at, and are less likely
to be convincing. Some writers think of the dialogue commercial as a
device for performing a verbal illustration without a visual demonstration.
Regardless of how you interpret the meaning of dialogue as a commercial
genre, it is basically a device for learning about a product.

The Demonstration Commercial

The *demonstration commercial* is a natural form of communication for television. Many think it is television's most useful genre. For example, it may be used to illustrate the versatility of a product or to show how a product or service is used, how it works, or what it does. This procedure is sometimes done with time-lapse photography. Many advertisers use the demonstration commercial for putting products and equipment through dramatic tests. These tests show the quality and superiority of a product or service over comparable brand products or services. This demonstration technique is often referred to as *torture testing*.

Before a writer begins constructing a demonstration commercial, considerable research and sometimes actual trial-and-error testing is necessary. The writer does not always do the research or testing, but the writer should be present to see the testing so as to accumulate firsthand information and response to it.

Although most commercials use words at the rate of approximately 150 words per minute, demonstration commercials use 80 to 100 words per minute. The fewer the number of words, the more time there will be for the viewer to concentrate on the visual aspects of the commercial. In general, talk is used only as a needed supplement to fill in and explain what is taking place during the demonstration.

During the production of a demonstration commercial the writer may need to develop and incorporate music and sound effects, or to work with a specialist in this field who is in charge of that aspect of production. These two kinds of audio, music and sound, are excellent communication devices. Music and sound can be used to create mood and help establish tone and a sense of reality. The presence of an adequate mood can mean the difference between success or failure of a demonstration commercial's ability to convince the viewer.

The Testimonial Commercial

One of the more useful and satisfactory ways of developing a *testimonial* about a product is to supply evidence of its effectiveness. This can be done by using a statement made by an individual who has had experience with the product or service. Such a statement, made by a witness, is a testimony concerning the benefits to be received. Testimonial statements are useful for products that are difficult to report on factually or measure scientifically. The testimonial is used with drugs and medications, as well as with intimate and personal products and services.

Examination of such testimonial statements indicates that they can be used almost any time. The following is an example:

(PERSON ON CAMERA SAYS): EVER SINCE I SWITCHED TO RIGHT FOOT
SHOES THEY MAKE MY FEET FEEL LIKE A PART OF MY BODY.

The Dramatized Commercial

The intent of every commercial is to communicate a message about a
product or service. The message must convince the listener-viewer that the
product or service will solve a specific problem, need, feeling, or desire. A
commercial form used widely today is the *dramatized commercial*.

The reason for its wide use is that it parallels reality by portraying an
event that involves people with a problem, need, feeling, or desire that
may involve removing spots, stains, dirt, or grime from clothes, floors, or
ceilings. It may be about how caffeine makes a person nervous or irritable.
It may be about how an individual's dentures do not stay in place. Or it
may be about how to get the most food value from your dollar. Whatever
the human problem, need, feeling, or desire, the solution involves the
product or service. Many times, it is recommended as the solution.

A dramatized commercial differs little from a play, except in length.
Basically it is developed around a single conflict. Usually two or more
individuals are involved.

The five-step process is especially adapted to helping the writer design
and develop the dramatized commercial. Because of its importance as a
specialized genre, this process and its use are discussed and illustrated in
Chapter 6.

The Production Commercial

This commercial may be of greater interest to the television producer or
director than it is to the television writer. Sometimes this commercial
requires little if any writing. And sometimes, because the *production
commercial* requires someone with an ability to write, produce, and direct,
its creation is the result of the combined efforts of several specialists.

While the production commercial takes on many characteristics, music
is generally used in its background. The writer may need the help of a
music specialist. Sometimes various sound effects or vocal music is a
requisite. On occasion the background for the scenes may consist of
floating landscapes, dancers, galloping horses, and other production
visuals. These diverse background settings mean that a team of specialists
frequently is needed in the creation of the production commercial.

Naturally, the product must be the focal point of each scene. That is
why this kind of commercial may have a vocal story line narrated
throughout. On occasion, however, the production commercial tells what
it has to say about the product entirely through sounds and visuals with a

quick verbal reference to the product at the end. It is evident that the creative potential of this form of commercial is limited only by the imagination of its creators and the budget limitation of its advertisers.

The Combination Commercial

Strictly speaking, this commercial is not a true genre but a combination of two or more kinds of commercials. The *combination commercial* must always work to the advantage of the product. For example, a combination commercial may even include a testimonial. Literally dozens of combinations can be created by a writer. After you become adept at writing each kind of commercial you should develop skill in taking advantage of the various combinations.

THE COMMERCIAL AND RADIO

There are a few specific conceptual differences between radio and television writing. These differences are primarily techniques and should be understood by the beginner before starting to write. First, radio is an audio medium. The language used must therefore create an adequate frame of reference in the listener's mind. It must do this regardless of where the listener may be or whatever he or she may be doing. For that reason, the writer's choice of words becomes the means with which the listener develops a mental image of the product or service. The writer's language, in addition to getting the listener's attention immediately, must create specific mental pictures in the listener's mind. Moreover, these images must help the listener see, smell, taste, and feel a total experience, a total understanding through the senses.

Because of this need, the beginning radio commercial writer must avoid all overworked words and phrases. Neither should the writer use superlatives nor trite radio patter. The superlatives you hear on the air are already overworked.

The beginning writer will also benefit from remembering that advertising agencies, as well as radio stations that write their own commercials, make every effort to present a quality of humanness. This approach should be a basic part of every beginning writer's style. Humanness is fundamental to the concept that in radio communication, you talk *with*, not *down to* or *at*, the listener.

A way to avoid talking down to the listener is to omit the *you* approach in writing. True, in some advertising messages, this use can be effective. But if a writer is not selective, the use of *you* can become offensive. The writer should be particularly careful about its use when the product is a part of the listener's daily routine—all those human experiences relating to dressing, grooming, health, and toilet habits. These human activites are personal and often traditional. They must be handled with verbal care.

To avoid falling into the habit of stirring up human defensiveness against a message, the writer can relate the product or service to the listener's universal desire for fuller living. (See the previously discussed five behavioral patterns and the use of synonyms.) The radio writer does this by using words that appeal to the listener's self-concept.

THE COMMERCIAL AND TELEVISION

Whereas radio is an audio medium, television is both audio and visual. As a result, the television writer has a greater choice of appeals. For example, when the listener-viewer is able to devote full visual attention to a commercial, that aspect of the commercial may be paramount. When this occurs, the verbal aspect is used primarily to supplement the visual.

When the listener-viewer is busy with other things, and by the very nature of what he or she is doing is a listener rather than a listener-viewer, the verbal aspect of a television message becomes paramount. It is then that the verbal must stimulate the mind through the ear, as it does in radio. It must create imagery essential to holding listener-viewer attention and interest.

Incidentally, many advertising agencies believe the ability to use visual imagery is so important that they insist new writers have radio commercial writing experience before they hire them. Be that as it may, the most important aspect of both radio and television writing is that the audio attention of the listener-viewer be caught and held.

Theoretically, television commercials have a communicative advantage over radio commercials because being able to both see and hear about a product or service is an approximation of being in its presence. It is thought by many that television can be even more specific than reality because the camera dispenses with peripheral distractions. What is seen via the camera is what you, the writer and producer, want the listener-viewer to see. Through this kind of selectivity, television moves the viewer closer to an action mode of response than can be done with language alone.

PLANNING THE COMMERCIAL

Time   Most time allotments for a commercial on the air are either 10, 20, 30, or 60 seconds. The writer begins constructing the commercial by thinking in terms of the amount of time that is available for its presentation.

Points   The next important step is to consider the number of specific points of interest about a product or service to be presented and discussed during the time available. Most writers and producers keep the number to a minimum. Practice seems to decree that one point of interest is psychologically better than two, provided that the one point is a good one.

Scenes   In a television commercial the writer also needs to consider how many camera scenes will be needed to develop the idea into an adequate story. A timing analysis of commercials indicates that one well-designed scene with adequate action and change in camera angles will sustain listener-viewer interest for 20 to 30 seconds. Timing measurements also indicate that human beings can psychologically focus their interest for 6 seconds or longer without a need for a change. Hence the time length of each scene must be carefully considered. The 6-second focus seems to be the minimum used in planning most commercial scenes.

General writing practices indicate that 10 to 15 seconds may be used in establishing the presence of a person who is to do a demonstration on television or make a major point about a product or service on radio.

Production practices in television indicate that most writers would do well to use no more than two camera shots for a 10-second commercial. As many as ten camera shots may be used, and are used, in a commercial that is 60 seconds long.

One general practice that you as a beginning commercial writer may want to try in the initial stage of your creativity is letting your instincts have free reign in the development of a commercial. After the idea, the procedure, the story line, the scenes, and the camera shots have been worked out, you then go back through what you have developed and rearrange it, step by step, to fit a specific process pattern. After this revision, you place your emphasis on writing and on the production techniques needed to increase the communicating strength of the completed commercial.

READINESS IN WRITING

First, the copywriter should know certain aspects of performance, including the use of voice. These skills should apply to the writer as well as others because in many stations the writer does his or her own voicing.

Second, the copywriter must understand certain aspects of production and how these may be used to reinforce what is being communicated with the voice and body.

Third, the copywriter must understand and control his or her writing talent. Ready-made talent varies from person to person. It is the purpose of this text to help you discover yours and develop each facet of your ability.

Fourth, while the processes explained here will help you learn *how* to write, another procedure that is essential to every writer's success is knowing how to develop background material that will help you understand the purpose and intent of the product or service. Such information is essential before you begin writing.

THE FACT-FINDER

The *fact-finder* is designed to help you collect the data and information essential to developing a background and an understanding of a specific product or service. Those who use it have found it to be a shortcut to developing a *fact sheet*, which is a collection of specific information for writing the commercial.

As every experienced writer knows, discovering adequate facts about a product or service can be an onerous and seemingly endless task. Below are eight steps that will speed up your efforts. As you gain experience and develop your intuition, you may add steps of your own, combine some of these steps, or eliminate some.

Product or Service   Under this heading list the name of the product or service, classify it, list the manufacturer and identify the distributor, and jot down other pertinent facts that help identify the product or service.

Personal Experience   Under this step the copywriter recalls and recounts personal experiences that relate to this product or service, or to similar ones, as well as experiences of other individuals. These experiences can help creatively develop the commercial's thesis, theme, or central idea by showing how it relates to a specific problem, need, feeling, or desire. You will no doubt add to this basic information as you contemplate and search for additional information to meet the requirements of the remaining *fact-finder* steps. Remember that every commercial is linked to some human problem, need, feeling, or desire. A recent one is how to get dirt out of dark clothes when you cannot see that it is there.

Historical or Biographical Allusions   Information that links the product or service to a historical event (whether real or imagined) implies a direct reference or relationship between the product or service and the life of a well-known person. Sometimes the famous person is the talent for the commercial. Nonetheless, the information you list here may imply an important relationship to an event in history. The ripe coffee bean being picked by hand is an example. Some of the information you collect for this step may later be used as a causal reference, a cause-to-effect relationship.

Research and Statistical Data   The information collected under this item should be facts developed by researchers and experimenters. Such facts should relate to and help verify the point of view expressed in your initial statement. ("More doctors recommend XYZ than any other product.") This information may come from the manufacturer's laboratories, experiments, or other research laboratory sources.

Reference to Authority   Under this category include citations from authorities qualified to make a statement about the product or service. Authorities may include authors, researchers, or other experts in their fields. This is a widely used technique.

Causal Relationships   Under this heading place all materials and information that can be used in developing a cause-to-effect rationale. A causal relationship implies or expresses a correlation between a cause and the effect it has. ("Four out of five dog owners prefer XX brand dog food. Shouldn't your dog have XX?")

Analogies   The term *analogy* implies that if two or more things agree with one another in some respect, there will most likely be agreements in other ways. When two ideas or events have likenesses, that fact permits the writer to draw an analogy. List as many analogies as you can discover for your product or service. Naturally you will not use them all. But list several because one might prove to be a more useful analogy when you get around to writing.

Comparison and Contrast   A contrast is the difference between two objects, ideas, or concepts. A comparison is always made between things, events, people, happenings. It is accomplished by bringing them together in order to point out likenesses. Contrasts are made for the purpose of discovering differences. These differences are arrived at by placing things together so that dissimilarities may be pointed out. This technique is used by several network advertisers.

Summary of Fact Finding

The fact-finder has, through use, demonstrated that it is an exceptionally useful procedure to follow in getting ready to write a commercial. It helps the writer consider a product or service from a wide perspective. Although you may not be able to use every category every time, the many-sided approach makes for a more objective consideration of the product or service.

The specific development of any commercial will in part be determined by the subject matter and the air time available. If the commercial is to be 30 seconds, certain steps in the fact-finder may be more helpful than others. A 10-second time limit may demand other categories.

Finally, it is an assumption worth considering that the more commercials you write, the closer you will come to being intuitive about the entire writing process. Experience gained from successful writing, like that gained from successfully driving a car, will help you develop your intuition if you are willing to discipline yourself and follow specific learning routines. Every beginning copywriter should be reminded that the process of writing cannot be learned or acquired by living and working in a vacuum. Writing ability comes from following writing routines. Never indulge yourself by "taking time to commence to get ready to start." When you sit down to write, go to work.

PART II

WRITING

CHAPTER 5

Writing the Radio and Television Commercial

THE PROCESS APPROACH

The purpose of a commercial message is to gain listener-viewer attention and produce a positive decoding feedback; that is, to get the consumer to buy the product or use the service. Copy that fulfills this function usually begins with a factual statement, observation, opinion, contention, or reaction to something or someone. This not only catches the listener-viewer's attention but serves as a thesis, theme, or central idea for the entire message. For example:

> WHIRLPOOL HAS BEEN HIDING SOMETHING BEHIND THESE NO
> FINGERPRINT DOORS.

This initial statement both catches attention and implies a thesis, theme, or central idea. The writer then follows with a statement that relates the first statement to a problem, need, feeling, or desire.

> A LOT OF PEOPLE BOUGHT OUR REFRIGERATORS JUST BECAUSE OF THE
> WAY THEY RESIST FINGERPRINTS. BUT LOOK INSIDE AT THE

67

ADJUSTABLE SHELVING, THE PORCELAIN ENAMELED INTERIORS, THE
COMPLETE ICE SYSTEM. YOU'LL FIND MORE THAN GREAT
REFRIGERATOR DOORS. YOU'LL FIND THE KIND OF CONVENIENCE,
THE KIND OF QUALITY, THAT MAKES WHIRLPOOL, WHIRLPOOL.

These informative details assure the listener-viewer that the relationship between the thesis, theme, or central idea and the problem, need, feeling, or desire can be taken care of by using the product. The copywriter then makes a final statement whose purpose is to motivate the listener-viewer into becoming a consumer. The final statement is a prognostication, a conclusion, an objective judgment, or a suggestion implying that the product will do the job because it is reputable and reliable, and therefore worth possessing. Sometimes *when* and *where* the product or service may be purchased is included. The Whirlpool commercial concludes with the simple, straightforward statement:

BECAUSE QUALITY IS OUR WAY OF LIFE.[1]

This brief analysis demonstrates *why* a commercial is constructed as it is. Experience indicates that this formula seems to be the surest way to get the "'selling'" job done. This analysis does not give the beginning copywriter specific procedures in *how* to write. For this purpose, a step-by-step process is needed. The processes explained in this chapter are just that. Before you can begin writing, however, you must have something to write about.

DEVELOPING DATA FOR WRITING A COMMERCIAL

Most writers follow six procedural steps when preparing to write a commercial.

1. *The writer collects all the information available about a product or service.* The most efficient way to collect this information is to use the eight-part fact-finder in Chapter 4. The usual information sources are the manufacturer, the supplier, the distributor, the sales outlet, and reliable references and data sources.

Sometimes all of these sources plus consumer experience must be used. If you are working for a local station, then most of your information will come from the advertiser, the person offering the particular product or service for sale. In fact, the advertiser and the consumer are frequently the only sources available to you.

For example, if radio or television time is purchased by a local carpet

1. Courtesy Whirlpool Co., J. D. Clever, Natural Advertising Manager, Benton Harbor, Michigan.

shop, then as a writer you will most likely talk with the carpet shop's manager or representative. The same is true if the advertising time is solicited by such advertisers as a grocery market, a jewelry store, a specialty shop, a car dealer, or a service station.

In some broadcast outlets the information needed about a product or service is brought to the copywriter by the *time salesman.* In general, however, the time salesman is too busy interviewing potential advertisers and selling time to help with fact finding. This means you must discover your own sources to collect the information you need.

Occasionally the information is prepared by the advertiser's office. Sometimes, on the local scene, it is hundreds of words plus the request that it all be used in 30 seconds. When this occurs, you have a special problem that can be solved only through diplomacy.

If you are working for a large station that writes and produces commercials for advertisers, the preparation routine may be quite different. Certainly the routine in an advertising agency is different. And all routines change from time to time.

Practical experience dictates that for the present we should concentrate primarily on preparations that are essential to learning how to write copy. Therefore, regardless of the source from which information for copy is obtained, you will discover that some commercials can be written with just a few facts. Other commercials need a lot of information, if for nothing more than to give the writer adequate background.

After the information is gathered, organize it and check it for accuracy and consistency in terms of the particular product. Then take the information you need from your fact-finder and create a *fact sheet.* It is called this because it is a series of statements, facts about the product or service that are the subject of the commercial. The length of each fact sheet is in general determined by the amount of information available and may have little to do with how long the commercial is to be.

The following examples of fact sheets were created by a commercial copywriter. Read each fact sheet to see if the details are adequate for you. They were for this commercial copywriter, but then Mr. Anonymous had years of experience and possessed a special understanding of listener-viewer self-image in his area. Nevertheless, what he knew and used there in all probability would not have been useful in another market.

Examples of Fact Sheets

- Christmas Party (annual).
  Host: Phiffer Bakeries, East Avenue and 24th Street.
  Sunday, December 19, 4:00 P.M. to 6:00 P.M.
  Santa Claus will give hot Phiffer bread and butter to all children.

Children must be accompanied by parents!!!!
There will be prizes, balloons, candy.
See the giant Christmas tree at East Avenue and 24th Street, Centertown.

- William's boneless Turkey Roast.
  Perfect slices, because of William's perfect slicing.
  No crumbling, strings, or bones.
  White meat, or white and dark meat combinations.
  Comes frozen in its own roaster.
  Bastes itself and makes plenty of juice for gravy.
  Serves six to eight people.

- Typewriter shop.
  Fast, friendly service.
  Money-back guarantee.
  Nearly all makes and models: Royal, Olympia, Underwood, Smith-Corona, others.
  Repairs guaranteed.
  Teddy's Typewriter Shop, 1801 Mondale Street, Centertown.

2. *The writer must understand the purpose of the commercial.* For example, the writer should know:

- Is this to be the first ad in a series?
- Is the ad to sell a specific product or service, or several?
- Is the ad to increase the sales of an ongoing product or service?
- Is the ad to develop a more favorable attitude or opinion of the product, service, or the company?
- Is the ad to develop a point of view in an effort to help the company gain a larger share of the available market?

3. *The writer must develop a strategic plan.* This means the writer needs to determine who the potential users of the product or service are. Therefore, the copywriter consults with the advertiser in an effort to learn what group or groups of listener-viewers the advertiser wishes to reach. You in turn will consult the available demographic reports for the area to discover the following basic details. On occasion you may need additional information.

- What is the general age of potential users?
- What seems to be their maturity and social status?
- What is the ethnic background of potential users?
- What is the economic level, the income average, of potential customers?

- Is a special customer, *a key customer*, important in the writing of this particular commercial?

4. *The writer must determine the appeals to be used in the commercial.* Knowing the appeals to be used helps the writer decide which creative approach to use. Specifically, the writer should review the collected information about the product or service to determine whether there is something unique about it that can be featured as a solution to a problem, need, feeling, or desire. In reaching a decision the writer should determine:

- How the product or service is distinctly different from its competition.
- What outstanding feature about it may be used to appeal to the potential listener-viewer.
- What secondary feature can be used as an appeal to the listener-viewer.

These answers will help the copywriter determine the kind of appeal to make to the listener-viewers' *six* senses. The senses selected for use are basically determined by the product's or the service's appearance, performance, economy, durability, safety, and comfort characteristics.

5. *The writer must think of the product in terms of the media on which the commercial is to be aired.* In general the information the writer has compiled up to this point should determine:

- Whether the information about the product will communicate better on radio, on television, or on both.
- What time of day the message should be aired for best results.
- Which specific human appeals about the product or service can best be used.
- Whether these appeals should be presented as facts, general information, human interest, conflict, humor, unique features, self-concept, specific sensations, feelings, sexual interest, or a combination of these.
- What type of commercial will best communicate with the targeted listener-viewer? Many times, the cost of production determines the kind of commercial that will be used. Production costs often decree that the *straight* commercial be used. This is true for both radio and television, especially on local stations. On the local scene many businesses cannot afford commercials similar to those on the networks.

6. *The writer now creates a message fulfilling the requirements established in the five previous steps.* Let us see how this is accomplished by going through each of the six points and writing a commercial for a client whose name is Lee Drugs. The client is located in the Maple Leaf Mall. Suppose you work for a local advertising agency. One of the time salesmen brought in a contract for a 30-second spot that is to be used on both radio and television. Your job is to write the copy. The production department will take over from there. Here's how to begin:

Secure all the information that you can about the product or service. The first thing you do is use the fact-finder so you can prepare a fact sheet. You begin this procedure by meeting with the Lee Drug manager. From him you learn he wants to advertise a new pen. It is the Elwell Gold Pen. You therefore use each step in the fact-finder and based on what you are able to discover, develop the following fact sheet.

Elwell Gold Pen.
Fourteen Kt. gold point, elegant, with a classic look.
$35, manufacturer's suggest retail price.
Lifetime guarantee.
Retractable point.
High-quality, ball-point cartridge.
Has a panel for engraving.
Refillable.
Manufactured by Elwell and Company, which has been in business
    since 1864.

Next you discover the purpose of the proposed commercial. Your efforts produced the following: Lee Drug wants to introduce this pen as a means of creating a traffic flow through its store. The traffic flow that Lee Drug wants is people who can afford a $35 pen. Lee Drug has redone the interior of its store and wants more affluent customers to visit it. They believe that once these people see their store, they will return and become customers. The first commercial is to run for ten days.

Next you decide on a strategic plan for presenting the commercial. This step produces information that you will be able to develop into an overall course of action. For example, Lee Drug wants the commercial to appeal to heads of households, both wives and husbands. In addition, the manager wants to attract customers interested in quality merchandise. This means that the socioeconomic level of the listener-viewer has already been decided upon. The message you write must appeal specifically to that level.

You need to determine the appeals to be used in the commercial. The information you collect for this step causes you to realize that you must definitely appeal to each listener-viewer's self-concept of status and personal prestige. The information you collected with the fact-finder is of specific help. After all, the Elwell Gold Pen is 14-karat. It literally has no competition. It is a fine, elegant pen. What you must say about it is becoming clear.

Next you need to determine the specific media presentation to be used. This decision has already been made for you. The commercial is to run simultaneously on radio and television. That means your copy must lend itself to being communicated audibly and visually. On radio the commercial is to be heard at noon and in the evening by commuters on their way home. The commercial on local television is to catch the housewife's attention after her husband has gone to work and the children are off to school. It is also to be telecast during the noon hour and again with the six o'clock news. As a dual commercial it is to be aired for ten days with possible updating and changes.

The Lee Drug advertising budget determines the kind of commercial you will write. Most of the money is to be used buying time. Therefore you will write a *straight* commercial.

Now you are to write a message fulfilling the requirements in the previous five steps. Before you begin writing the commercial, review all the information you have collected. Immediately you know there are certain fundamentals essential to this commercial that must be kept in mind. First, because it is a short commercial, you probably should limit it to a single appeal. This appeal you will reiterate in as many different ways as possible without sounding too repetitious. You will also need to add as much meaningful information to the single appeal as possible.

The *six-step process* will help you accomplish this. It will also help you identify the product with the listener-viewer's self-concept.

A short commercial like this one must be concise and clear. It must also be as direct and as personal as the subject matter and the demographics will permit. The six-step process will help you with that problem.

HOW TO USE THE SIX-STEP PROCESS

STEP 1—INITIAL STATEMENT

By the very nature of a commercial, the initial statement, the *lead*, is based on and determined by the purpose and intent of the message. This initial statement should state or imply a thesis, theme, or central idea that will help solve a problem, fulfill a need, or satisfy a feeling or a desire. Moreover, this lead statement should catch the listener-viewer's attention. Specifically, this initial statement must cause the listener-viewer to become aware that what is being said involves his or her self-concept. As a result of hearing the initial statement the listener-viewer will want to know more about the product or service.

After reviewing all the material in the fact sheet about the Elwell pen and Lee Drug, you write several trial leads and decide on this one:

YOU CAN WRITE WITH ANY PEN, BUT YOU WRITE IN STYLE WITH AN
ELWELL.

STEP 2—REPETITION-REINFORCEMENT STATEMENT
The content of the second step must repeat the original thought in different words. By developing the opening of the commercial this way, Step 2 reinforces the initial statement and creates interest in the product or service. It does this by reaffirming the suggested way of fulfilling the implied or stated thesis, theme, or central idea in Step 1 as it relates to a problem, need, feeling, or desire. Therefore Step 2 increases the listener-viewer's desire to hear more about the product or service.

After reviewing the fact sheet and rereading what you have written for Step 1, and after a few trials, you write:

AN ELWELL PEN HAS THE ELEGANCE AND QUALITY OF A FINE
WRITING INSTRUMENT.

Before going on, you read Steps 1 and 2 together to see how they sound.

YOU CAN WRITE WITH ANY PEN, BUT YOU WRITE IN STYLE WITH AN
ELWELL. AN ELWELL PEN HAS THE ELEGANCE AND QUALITY OF A
FINE WRITING INSTRUMENT.

STEP 3—TRANSITIONAL STATEMENT
This step prepares the listener-viewer for a fuller explanation and elaboration of Step 1's thesis, theme, or central idea as it relates to a problem, need, feeling, or desire that is being implied or stated.

Again you review your data, reread what you have written, and write:

IT IS THE UTMOST IN STYLE AND SATISFACTION.

Now you put everything you have written together by reading it to hear how it sounds.

YOU CAN WRITE WITH ANY PEN, BUT YOU WRITE IN STYLE WITH AN
ELWELL. AN ELWELL PEN HAS THE ELEGANCE AND QUALITY OF A
FINE WRITING INSTRUMENT. IT IS THE UTMOST IN STYLE AND
SATISFACTION.

STEP 4—VISUALIZATION STATEMENT
In this step you need to visualize the thesis, theme, or central ideas as it relates to a problem, need, feeling, or desire that you believe is held by the listener-viewer. You do this by suggesting a way or ways in which the

listener-viewer's interest in what is said in Step 1 can be visualized. The statement you write must help the listener-viewer understand why the proposal in Step 1, reinforced in Step 2 and 3, is believable and the product desirable.

You review your fact sheet and write:

FROM THE FOURTEEN KARAT GOLD BODY TO THE PRECISION TIPPED
BALL POINT, AN ELWELL PEN GIVES A LIFETIME OF SERVICE.

Now you reread what you have written:

YOU CAN WRITE WITH ANY PEN, BUT YOU WRITE IN STYLE WITH AN
ELWELL. AN ELWELL PEN HAS THE ELEGANCE AND QUALITY OF A
FINE WRITING INSTRUMENT. IT IS THE UTMOST IN STYLE AND
SATISFACTION. FROM THE FOURTEEN KARAT GOLD BODY TO THE
PRECISION TIPPED BALL POINT, AN ELWELL PEN GIVES A LIFETIME OF
SERVICE.

STEP 5—SATISFACTION STATEMENT

The content of this step must help the listener-viewer experience and enjoy the satisfaction of understanding, accepting, believing, possessing, or doing that which has been implied or suggested in the previous four statements.

Again you read what you have written to get a feel of how the language *flows*. Then you study the fact sheet and in terms of what you need in step 5 you write:

THAT IS WHY AN ELWELL PEN ADDS A NEW DIMENSION TO WRITING,
AND A CLASSIC TOUCH TO ANY DESK, ATTACHÉ CASE, OR POCKET.

After that statement, designed to help the listener-viewer feel pleased about the prospect of owning an Elwell Pen, you are ready to conclude your commercial.

STEP 6—ACTION OR RESULT STATEMENT

This final statement must suggest the action the listener-viewer should take or the reaction the listener-viewer should experience by responding positively to the thesis, theme, or central idea as it relates to a listener-viewer's problem, need, feeling, or desire that you implied or stated earlier. This statement must do just that by fulfilling and satisfying the basic self-concept that has been awakened in the listener-viewer.

In order to write this final statement for your commercial, you reread all you have written and review the fact sheet. Step 6 can be a simple, straightforward statement suggesting an action. Therefore you write:

TO SEE AND INSPECT THIS FINE WRITING INSTRUMENT, THE ELWELL
PEN, VISIT LEE DRUG IN THE MAPLE LEAF MALL.

You now need to check how your completed commercial looks on paper
and test how it sounds to the ear of someone. How it will look on television
is for production to decide. Therefore you type out a copy and read it aloud
as you check it for time and melody. If there are rhythmic problems with
the language, you correct these step by step. If the commercial is too short,
you discover where you can add to the content. If it is too long, you rewrite
by condensing. Remember, it is usually better to overwrite and condense
(cut) than underwrite and have to pad. Specificity is more easily achieved
by overwriting and cutting. Here is how the Elwell Pen commercial looks
on paper:

YOU CAN WRITE WITH ANY PEN, BUT YOU WRITE IN STYLE WITH AN
ELWELL. AN ELWELL PEN HAS THE ELEGANCE AND QUALITY OF A
FINE WRITING INSTRUMENT. IT IS ALSO THE UTMOST IN STYLE AND
SATISFACTION. FROM THE FOURTEEN KARAT GOLD BODY TO THE
PRECISION TIPPED BALL POINT, AN ELWELL PEN GIVES A LIFETIME OF
SERVICE. THAT IS WHY AN ELWELL PEN ADDS A NEW DIMENSION TO
WRITING, AND A CLASSIC TOUCH TO ANY DESK, ATTACHÉ CASE, OR
POCKET. TO SEE AND INSPECT THIS FINE WRITING INSTRUMENT, THE
ELWELL PEN, VISIT LEE DRUG IN THE MAPLE LEAF MALL.

Let us next see how the Whirlpool commercial reprinted at the
beginning of this chapter can be diagramed by following the six-step
process.

STEP 1—INITIAL STATEMENT
WHIRPOOL HAS BEEN HIDING SOMETHING BEHIND THESE NO
FINGEPRINT DOORS.

STEP 2—REPETITION-REINFORCEMENT STATEMENT
A LOT OF PEOPLE BOUGHT OUR REFRIGERATORS JUST BECAUSE OF THE
WAY THEY RESISTED FINGERPRINTS.

STEP 3—TRANSITIONAL STATEMENT
BUT LOOK INSIDE

STEP 4—VISUALIZATION STATEMENT
AT THE ADJUSTABLE SHELVING, THE PROCELAIN ENAMELED
INTERIORS, THE COMPLETE ICE SYSTEM.

STEP 5—SATISFACTION STATEMENT
YOU'LL FIND MORE THAN GREAT REFRIGERATOR DOORS. YOU'LL FIND

THE KIND OF CONVENIENCE, THE KIND OF QUALITY, THAT MAKES
WHIRLPOOL, WHIRLPOOL.

STEP 6—ACTION OR RESULT STATEMENT
BECAUSE QUALITY IS OUR WAY OF LIFE.[2]

You will have noted by this time that the six-step writing process is adaptable to commercial copywriting because it begins with a factual statement and through repetition, visualization, and description, develops an appeal to the listener-viewer's self-concept.

After you have written a commercial, always read it aloud. As you do, be sure to listen for secondary meanings, feelings, and attitudes. These will all be missed if you listen only to the thoughts as you read. Be objective and hear what is being said. When you hear verbal distractions, change or cut them from your copy. It is singleness of purpose that will assure listener-viewer response. Reading your commercial aloud to others is even more helpful.

As you continue using the six-step process you will discover it works best most of the time in its entirety because each step flows into or combines with the next step. This means you can often improve the commercial by joining the thoughts in two or more steps. This is particularly true in commercials that by their nature are no more than two or three sentences long. Note how Steps 3 and 4 are combined in the Whirlpool commercial.

For other examples, see the following commercials. The first one is twenty-eight words long. Note how the individual steps combine to create a succinct message.

Example 1

STEP 1—INITIAL STATEMENT
SELL YOUR WRECKED CAR TO TONY.

STEP 2—REINFORCEMENT STATEMENT
TONY BUYS

STEP 3—TRANSITIONAL STATEMENT
ALL MAKES AND MODELS

STEP 4—VISUALIZATION STATEMENT
TO GET SALVAGE PARTS.

2. Courtesy Whirlpool Co., J. D. Clever, National Adverstising Manager, Benton Harbor, Michigan.

STEP 5—SATISFACTION STATEMENT
TONY ALSO HANDLES NEW PARTS.

STEP 6—ACTION OR RESULT STATEMENT
SEE TONY'S SALVAGE SHOP, EAST TENTH, STILLVILLE.

Here is how the commercial appeared to the announcer.

> SELL YOUR WRECKED CAR TO TONY. TONY BUYS ALL MAKES AND
> MODELS TO GET SALVAGE PARTS. TONY ALSO HANDLES NEW PARTS.
> SEE TONY'S SALVAGE SHOP, EAST TENTH, STILLVILLE.

Example 2

STEP 1—INITIAL STATEMENT
PAINT YOUR HOME ECONOMICALLY WITH MOLLY-PITCHER QUALITY
HOUSE PAINT

STEP 2—REINFORCEMENT STATEMENT
DURING CLEAN-UP, FIX-UP, PAINT-UP WEEK IN TOWNVILLE.

STEP 3—TRANSITIONAL STATEMENT
SEE OR CALL HAL GREEN AT TOWNVILLE'S PAINT AND SUPPLIES FOR
PRICES AND ESTIMATES.

STEP 4—VISUALIZATION STATEMENT
HAL GREEN WILL EXPLAIN HOW MOLLY-PITCHER HOUSE PAINT
RESISTS MILDEW.

STEP 5—SATISFACTION STATEMENT
LEARN HOW MOLLY-PITCHER HOUSE PAINT DOES A BETTER JOB.

STEP 6—ACTION OR RESULT STATEMENT
YOU WILL FIND EVERY PAINT YOU NEED AT TOWNVILLE'S PAINT AND
SUPPLIES NEW LOCATION, TEN EAST NINTH STREET.

Here is the commercial as it appeared to the announcer:

> PAINT YOUR HOME ECONOMICALLY WITH MOLLY-PITCHER QUALITY
> HOUSE PAINT DURING CLEAN-UP, FIX-UP, PAINT-UP WEEK IN
> TOWNVILLE. SEE OR CALL HAL GREEN AT TOWNVILLE'S PAINT AND
> SUPPLIES FOR PRICES AND ESTIMATES. HAL GREEN WILL EXPLAIN
> HOW MOLLY-PITCHER HOUSE PAINT RESISTS MILDEW. LEARN HOW

MOLLY-PITCHER HOUSE PAINT DOES A BETTER JOB. YOU WILL FIND
EVERY PAINT YOU NEED AT TOWNVILLE'S PAINT AND SUPPLIES NEW
LOCATION, TEN EAST NINTH STREET.

The Six-Step Process and the Television Commercial

One way to understand how the six-step process can be used in television
copywriting is to diagram several commercials. Tape the copy, type it, and
then diagram it. Diagraming helps one understand the relationship between the six-step process and the creative procedure. Your diagram
should be similar to the following.

Television Example 1

VIDEO	AUDIO

STEP 1—INITIAL STATEMENT (thesis, theme, central idea as it relates to a
problem, need, feeling, or desire).

CLOSE-UP OF GRACE JEWEL, DENTURE WEARER, ON HIDEN CAMERA.	ANNCR: (VO) WHY DID GRACE JEWEL STOP USING HER CREAM DENTURE ADHESIVE?

STEP 2—REPETITION-REINFORCEMENT STATEMENT

GRACE JEWEL	GRACE: IT OOZED OUT AROUND THE SIDES OF MY DENTURES.

STEP 3—TRANSITIONAL STATEMENT

CLOSE-UP OF DENTURE POWDER BOX AND PLATES BEING SPRAYED WITH FASTEETH POWDER	ANNCR: (VO) WE ASKED HER TO TRY THE NATURAL POWER ADHESIVE . . . FASTEETH POWDER. IT SPRAYS ON IN A SMOOTH EVEN LAYER.

STEP 4—VISUALIZATION STATEMENT

GRACE JEWEL, PRODUCT, PACKAGE ON TABLE BEFORE HER.	GRACE: I HAVE NO PROBLEM WITH ANY OOZING AT ALL OVER THE EDGE. MY DENTURES NOW FEEL LIKE THEY'RE A NATURAL PART OF MY MOUTH. IT'S THAT EASE, THAT FEEL OF BEING ABLE TO DO WHAT YOU WANT TO DO WITHOUT BEING EMBARRASSED.

STEP 5—SATISFACTION STATEMENT

VIDEO	AUDIO
CLOSE-UP OF PACKAGE.	ANNCR: (VO) FASTEETH POWDER MAKES DENTURES FEEL MORE LIKE YOUR OWN TEETH.

STEP 6—ACTION OR RESULT STATEMENT

VIDEO	AUDIO
GRACE JEWEL ON SPLIT SCREEN WITH PRODUCT.	GRACE: LIKE THEY'RE A NATURAL PART OF YOUR MOUTH NOW.[3]

Television Example 2

VIDEO	AUDIO

STEP 1—INITIAL STATEMENT

VIDEO	AUDIO
CLOSE-UP OF HANDS WORKING ON CARB OR SPARK PLUGS. PULL BACK TO REVEAL MECHANIC UNDER HOOD OF CAR IN TUNE-UP GARAGE.	ANNCR: MIKE MCDONALD HAS BEEN WORKING ON AUTOMOBILE ENGINES FOR 18 YEARS.

STEP 2—REPETITION-REINFORCEMENT STATEMENT

VIDEO	AUDIO
	ANNCR: YOU KNOW WHEN HE'S FINISHED YOU'VE RECEIVED THE BEST EXPERTISE MONEY CAN BUY.

STEP 3—TRANSITIONAL STATEMENT

VIDEO	AUDIO
FLIP PAGE TO ANNCR. IN STUDIO OFFICE, SITTING ON EDGE OF DESK.	THE SAME IS TRUE AT FIRST FEDERAL SAVINGS OF PANAMA CITY.

STEP 4—VISUALIZATION STATEMENT

VIDEO	AUDIO
VIDIFONT: FIRST FEDERAL SAVINGS.	(VO) OUR COUNSELORS ARE THOROUGHLY TRAINED TO INSURE YOU RECEIVE PROFESSIONAL ADVICE ON SAVING FOR THE FUTURE. PEOPLE, LIKE ENGINES, ARE DIFFERENT, AND WHAT'S GOOD FOR ONE MAY NOT BE RIGHT FOR ANOTHER.

3. Courtesy Malcolm S. MacGruer, Director-Corporate Communications Richardson-Vics, Inc., Wilton, Connecticut.

B&B

BENTON & BOWLES
909 THIRD AVENUE
NEW YORK, N Y
(212) 758-6200

Client: VICK CHEMICAL CO.
Product: FASTEETH
Length: 30 SECONDS—(RXFP9013)
Title: "GRACE JEWELL II"

ANNCR: (VO) Why did Grace Jewell stop using her cream denture adhesive?

GRACE: It oozed out around the sides of my dentures.

ANNCR: (VO) We asked her to try the natural powder adhesive...Fasteeth powder.

It sprays on

in a smooth even layer.

GRACE: I have no problem with any oozing at all over the edge.

My dentures now feel like they're a natural part of my mouth.

It's that ease, that feeling of

being able to do what you want to do

without being embarrassed.

ANNCR: (VO) Fasteeth powder makes dentures feel more like your own teeth.

GRACE: Like they're a natural part of your mouth now.

Courtesy Benton and Bowles

STEP 5—SATISFACTION STATEMENT

SLOW ZOOM IN ON ANNCR.

ANNCR: WHEN YOU START A SAVINGS PROGRAM AT FIRST FEDERAL SAVINGS, YOU CAN BE SURE IT'S BEEN FINE TUNED FOR GOOD PERFORMANCE, FOR YOUR SPECIAL NEEDS.

STEP 6—ACTION OR RESULT STATEMENT

ZOOM BACK AND BRING IN SHOT OF MECHANIC FROM EARLIER SCENE.
VIDIFONT: FIRST FEDERAL SAVINGS 6 CONVENIENT LOCATIONS IN PANAMA CITY MEMBER FSLID.[4]

ANNCR: FIRST FEDERAL SAVINGS OF PANAMA CITY.

WHICH IS FIRST, WRITING OR PRODUCTION?

This is an important question to the beginning television commercial copywriter particularly if he or she has had considerable production experience. The answer is that when a commercial is basically production, you need to think in terms of the *video* first. Many television commercials depend on language to communicate their message. Some producers call these commercials "radio with pictures."

When the commercial depends primarily on words, many writers suggest that these commercials can be written before the production is planned. Most professionals say the issue is relative and meet the problem as it arises.

The following two commercials illustrate these differences. In the first one, the Whirlpool commercial, the video and production needs are made clear by the audio language. The second commercial depends primarily on production needs.

Example 1

VIDEO   AUDIO

STEP 1—INITIAL STATEMENT

ANNCR: WHIRLPOOL HAS BEEN HIDING SOMETHING BEHIND THESE NO FINGERPRINT DOORS.

---

4. Courtesy, Duane Franceschi, President, Financial Marketing Concepts, Tallahassee, Florida.

STEP 2—REPETITION-REINFORCEMENT STATEMENT

A LOT OF PEOPLE BOUGHT OUR
REFRIGERATORS JUST BECAUSE OF
THE WAY THEY RESISTED
FINGERPRINTS.

STEP 3—TRANSITIONAL STATEMENT

BUT LOOK INSIDE

STEP 4—VISUALIZATION STATEMENT

AT THE ADJUSTABLE SHELVING, THE
PROCELAIN ENAMELED INTERIOR,
THE COMPLETE ICE SYSTEM.

STEP 5—SATISFACTION STATEMENT

YOU'LL FIND MORE THAN GREAT
REFRIGERATOR DOORS. YOU'LL
FIND . . . THE KIND OF
CONVENIENCE, THE KIND OF
QUALITY THAT MAKES
WHIRLPOOL, WHIRLPOOL.

STEP 6—ACTION OR RESULT STATEMENT

BECAUSE QUALITY IS OUR WAY OF
LIFE.[5]

Example 2

Note the need for video details in the following commercial.

| VIDEO | AUDIO |

STEP 1—INITIAL STATEMENT

CHORUS: MAXWELL HOUSE IS COFFEE
TO WAKE UP TO. MAXWELL
HOUSE, "GOOD TO THE LAST
DROP."

STEP 2—REPETITION-REINFORCEMENT STATEMENT

MAXWELL HOUSE IS . . . MAXWELL
HOUSE IS . . .

5. Courtesy Whirlpool Co., J. D. Clever, National Advertising Manager, Benton Harbor, Michigan.

STEP 3—TRANSITIONAL STATEMENT

SGT: GOOD MORNING!
CHORUS: "GOOD TO THE LAST DROP,"
MAXWELL HOUSE.

STEP 4—VISUALIZATION STATEMENT

ANNCR: NOTHING GETS YOUR DAY
GOING . . . LIKE A CUP OF
MAXWELL HOUSE COFFEE.
COFFEE YOU CAN COUNT ON.
ALWAYS "GOOD TO THE LAST
DROP."

STEP 5—SATISFACTION STATEMENT

CHORUS: MAXWELL HOUSE IS . . .
MAN: A GOOD STARTER.

STEP 6—ACTION OR RESULT STATEMENT

CHORUS: "GOOD TO THE LAST DROP,"
MAXWELL HOUSE . . . [6]

THE STORYBOARD

Many copywriters, especially those in advertising agencies, use a story-board when they write a commercial. The storyboard is not only a visual to help stimulate the writer's imagination but can be used to illustrate the commercial for the client. For the beginning copywriter a storyboard can be a simple sketch placed within a line frame that is similar in shape to that of a television screen. In each framed space the copywriter sketches in a brief scene that is representative of a specific moment in the commercial. The beginner's storyboard should correlate with the steps in the process being used and the number of camera angles needed.

The use of a storyboard by a copywriter is similar to a miniature stage setting used by a beginning playwright. Beginning playwrights often build a miniature set so that they can move miniature characters through a scene before and after writing it to check the stage as the audience will see it. These movable characters are not necessarily realistic. Some playwrights use chessmen, and some use the cut-off tops of wooden clothespins.

Essentially the copywriter uses a storyboard to indicate the visual aspect of each camera shot and each scene when the camera angle is changed. You need adequate room beneath each storyboard frame you draw for writing down the audio and a description of what is taking place within the frame.

6. Courtesy Ogilvy & Mather Inc., New York, New York.

You do not need to be an artist to use a storyboard. Drawing stick-men or stick-women characters, or using your own pen or pencil invention, is adequate for developing and sketching audiovisual concepts.

Later, when you are "on the job," you may find that a storyboard is customary and frequently necessary in helping your peers visualize copy. There will be occasions when you will join forces with a specialist in the station's or the advertising agency's art department. This cooperative effort is especially helpful when professional copy is to be presented to a client before the commercial is shot.

ASSIGNMENTS: THE SIX-STEP COMMERCIAL

1. Be sure to use the step-by-step process to guide you. Identify each step before you write: for example, Step 1—Initial Statement. Doing so will remind you that the first statement in the commercial must state or imply a thesis, theme, or central idea that will help the listener-viewer solve a problem, fulfill a need, or satisfy a feeling or desire.

Follow this procedure for each step. Do not hesitate to turn back and review the definitions and explanations for each step. Habitually following this procedure stimulates and develops your imagination and ability.

2. Determine the socioeconomic status in your coverage area, decide on the products or services in which the listener-viewers will be most interested, and with the help of a fact-finder develop detailed fact sheets for at least five of the products or services you have listed.

3. Step by step until you develop fluency. Use a storyboard if you find it helpful.

- Write two 60-second commercials for radio.
- Write two 30-second commercials for radio.
- Write two 20-second commercials for radio.
- Write two 10-second commercials for radio.
- Write two 30-second commercials for radio and television.
- Write two 20-second commercials for radio and television.
- Write two 10-second commercials for radio and television.
- Write two 30-second commercials for television.
- Write two 20-second commercials for television.
- Write two 10-second commercials for television with emphasis on production.

Note: Be sure you have written two or more of each kind of commercial. See Chapter 4 for definitions of commercial types.

MODIFYING THE SIX-STEP COMMERCIAL

The basic concept of the six-step process may be used in a shortened form. You have already noted that a single statement may be divided into two steps. This was done in some of the illustrations, specifically in the Tony's Salvage commercial and the Townville Paint and Supplies ad.

Many times, the copywriter is assigned to write both a long and a short version of a commercial. You have no doubt heard such commercials on the air. Therefore, after you have had experience writing six-step process commercials, modify them. The modified or shortened version of the six-step process is especially useful for writing public service announcements (PSA's) and station indentifications (ID's).

PSA Example

STEP 1—INITIAL STATEMENT
THERE'S NOTHING MORE RELAXING THAN AN EVENING WALK.

STEP 3—TRANSITIONAL-STATEMENT
DINNER IS OVER, THE NEIGHBORHOOD IS QUIET, AND ONLY A FEW CARS CAN BE SEEN.

STEP 4—VISUALIZATION STATEMENT
BUT THERE IS A RIGHT AND A WRONG WAY TO WALK ALONG STREETS WITHOUT SIDEWALKS.

STEP 5—SATISFACTION STATEMENT
ALWAYS WALK FACING TRAFFIC SO YOU CAN SEE ALL VEHICLES THAT APPROACH YOU.

STEP 6—ACTION OR RESULT STATEMENT
WALKING IS HEALTHY IF YOU'RE CAREFUL. LEARN AND OBEY PEDESTRIAN SAFETY LAWS.[7]

ID Example

STEP 1—INITIAL STATEMENT
THIS IS C-N-N,

STEP 4—VISUALIZATION STATEMENT
CABLE NEWS NETWORK,

7. Courtesy Duane Franceschi, President, Financial Marketing Concepts, Tallahassee, Florida.

STEP 6—ACTION OR RESULT STATEMENT
THE TURNER BROADCASTING SYSTEM.[8]

HOW TO USE THE SEVEN-STEP PROCESS

The seven-step process presents details in a slightly different way from that found in the six-step process. Such a difference in commercial presentation is often necessary because products or services may need a development to match their differences.

Like the six-step process, the seven-step process can be used for either radio or television. All the writer needs to determine is which process can be used to an advantage. To make this decision the writer must have an adequate amount of information about the product or service. Data preparation is always an essential factor before beginning to write.

After you collect the information and prepare a fact sheet, you can begin thinking in terms of which writing process fits your information best. Determining which writing process is most useful is the same as determining which shoe goes on the right foot. Shape and fit are the determining factors.

For the purpose of learning to use the seven-step process, let us use a commercial that has appeared many times on television.

As you work with a process, develop a *feeling* for the specific use that can be made of each process step. Naturally, by the nature and intent of every commercial, Step 1 for the six-step and Step 1 for the seven-step process are much alike.

STEP 1—INITIAL STATEMENT

The intent of communicating a message presumes that the communicator begins by making an initial statement about a product or service that attracts the listener-viewer's attention. This initial statement is usually based on, or determined by, the purpose and intent of the message. As pointed out about Step 1 in the six-step process, the initial statement should embody or imply a thesis, theme, or central idea related to a problem, need, feeling, or desire. Moreover, Step 1 should be so conceived that it will catch the listener-viewer's attention and cause him or her to become aware that what is being said, or implied, is an idea, incident, situation, proposition, or objective *that relates to the listener-viewer's self-concept.* Therefore, he or she will want to hear more about the product or service. That is why Step 1, the initial statement in the Amana microwave oven commercial, begins with the following statement.

HERE'S ANOTHER FIRST FROM AMANA. . . .

8. Courtesy Turner Broadcasting System, Inc., Atlanta, Georgia.

STEP 2—REINFORCEMENT BY REPETITION

The second step in the seven-step process is similar to the second step in the six-step process. Through repetition, it adds clarity and force to the initial statement or reinforces it by suggesting or implying ways to fulfill the thesis, theme, or central idea as it relates to a problem, need, feeling, or desire. The second step in the Amana commercial does just that.

> A FIRST AND ONLY!

STEP 3—GIVES DETAILS OR EXAMPLES

The details or examples should illustrate the statement in Step 1 that was reinforced in Step 2. Note how the details listed in Step 3 of the Amana commercial explain Steps 1 and 2.

> AMANA IS THE FIRST AND ONLY MANUFACTURER OF MICROWAVE
> OVENS EXEMPTED FROM DISPLAYING THE U.S. GOVERNMENT SAFETY
> WARNING LABEL.

STEP 4—ASSIGNING ORIGIN OR CAUSE

The information in this step should explain the origin or cause for making the original thesis, theme, or central idea statement in Step 1, reinforced in Step 2, and detailed in Step 3. For example:

> THAT'S BECAUSE AFTER PASSING A SERIES OF VOLUNTARY TORTURE
> TESTS . . .

STEP 5—COMPARES THE CENTRAL IDEA WITH SIMILAR IDEAS OR PHE-NOMENA

The central idea (stated or implied in Step 1, reinforced in Step 2, detailed in Step 3, and assigned to an origin or cause in Step 4) should now be compared with a similar idea, object, situation, or principle. For example, the Amana commercial comparison is as follows:

> THE AMANA RADARANGE MICROWAVE OVEN DIDN'T JUST MEET
> FEDERAL SAFETY STANDARDS. IT EXCEEDED THEM.

STEP 6—CONTRAST CENTRAL IDEA WITH DISSIMILAR IDEAS OR PHENOMENA

The listener-viewer's interest in what is being talked about—the concept stated in Step 1, reinforced in Step 2, and developed according to the intent and purpose of Steps 3, 4, and 5—should now be contrasted with a dissimilar idea or phenomena. This is done to clarify the quality of the product and emphasize its superiority over similar products with which the listener-viewers may be familiar. Here is how it is done in the Amana commercial.

AND NO OTHER MANUFACTURER CAN MAKE THAT CLAIM.

STEP 7—ACTION OR PROGNOSTICATION STATEMENT
The final step in the seven-step process should prognosticate the results in whatever way is most appropriate to convince the listener-viewer. Of course Step 7 should be a fair and logical statement and not a value judgment. The Amana commercial concludes with a statement of fact.

REMEMBER, IF IT DOESN'T SAY AMANA, IT'S NOT A RADARANGE.

Below is the Amana commercial in its entirety. Read it several times, and insert the headline statement for each step as you read. Doing so is an excellent exercise in developing a feeling for using the seven-step process as a writing device.

HERE'S ANOTHER FIRST FROM AMANA.... A FIRST AND ONLY! AMANA
IS THE FIRST AND ONLY MANUFACTURER OF MICROWAVE OVENS
EXEMPT FROM DISPLAYING THE U.S. GOVERNMENT SAFETY WARNING
LABEL. THAT'S BECAUSE AFTER PASSING A SERIES OF VOLUNTARY
TORTURE TESTS. . . THE AMANA RADARANGE MICROWAVE OVEN
DIDN'T JUST MEET FEDERAL SAFETY STANDARDS. IT EXCEEDED
THEM. AND NO OTHER MANUFACTURER CAN MAKE THAT CLAIM.
REMEMBER, IF IT DOESN'T SAY AMANA, IT'S NOT A RADARANGE.[9]

ASSIGNMENTS: THE SEVEN-STEP COMMERCIAL

After you have had experience writing the six-step process, you will find using the seven-step process relatively easy. Be sure to include all seven steps. Use a storyboard if necessary. The same facts you developed for the six-step process may be used, or you may prepare new ones. The advantage in using the same data is that you discover how to write a different-style commercial. One former student wrote, "Thanks for the experience writing different commercials from the same basic data. How else would I handle these two similar million dollar accounts?"

Keep your commercials as brief as possible within the time limits.

1. Write two kinds of 30-second television commercials that require the use of each step in the seven-step process.

2. Write two kinds of 30-second radio commercials using all seven steps.

9. Courtesy Amana Refrigeration, Inc., Fred W. Streicher, National Advertising Manager, Amana, Iowa.

MODIFYING THE SEVEN-STEP PROCESS

As with the six-step process, it is not necessary to use every one of the steps in the seven-step process each time. The amount of information available, the nature of the data, and the length of the commercial usually determine the number of steps. Fundamentally, the length of a commercial will determine the number of words that will be used to make the message clear to the listener-viewer. The shorter the commercial, the less time the copywriter has in which to extend the evidence.

To comply with the time limit of a commercial, the copywriter may need to omit certain steps. For example, the writer may use Steps 1, 2, and 7 for an extremely short commercial. Or the writer may use Steps 1, 2, 3, 4, and 7. Almost any combination may be used if it helps the writer say what is needed about a product or service. Steps 1 and 7 will probably always be used.

A modified seven-step, because it lends itself to various combinations, is useful in writing ID's and PSA's. Listen to ID's and PSA's on the air, record some, and analyze them to discover what steps have been omitted.

Example 1, Steps 1, 2, 3, 7

STEP 1—INITIAL STATEMENT

TAKE THE WORRY OUT OF MOVING.

STEP 2—REINFORCEMENT-REPETITION

CONTACT P AND L TRANSFER AND STORAGE COMPANY.

STEP 3—DETAILS OR EXAMPLES

YOUR HOUSEHOLD GOODS ARE HANDLED SAFELY BY DEPENDABLE WORKMEN WITH FAST, SURE VANS.

STEP 7—ACTION OR PROGNOSTICATION STATEMENT

TO MOVE OR TO STORE YOUR POSSESSIONS, CALL P AND L, AGENTS FOR BAKER VAN LINES, INCORPORATED. TELEPHONE P AND L, 555-2222.

Here is how the shortened seven-step looks to the announcer:

TAKE THE WORRY OUT OF MOVING. CONTACT P AND L TRANSFER AND STORAGE COMPANY. YOUR HOUSEHOLD GOODS ARE HANDLED SAFELY BY DEPENDABLE WORKMEN WITH FAST, SURE VANS. TO MOVE OR TO STORE YOUR POSSESSIONS, CALL P AND L, AGENTS FOR BAKER VAN LINES, INCORPORATED. TELEPHONE P AND L, 555-2222.

Example 2, Steps 1, 2, 3, 5, 7 (for radio)

STEP 1—INITIAL STATEMENT
FIR DIMENSIONS FOR SPRING REPAIR WORK

STEP 2—REINFORCEMENT-REPETITION
ARE NOW ON SPECIAL SALE AT MARTIN'S LUMBER COMPANY, 1200
WEST SIXTH.

STEP 3—GIVES DETAILS OR EXAMPLES
BUY WHILE YOU CAN SAVE: 2 BY 4S, 2 BY 6S, AT 20 PERCENT DISCOUNT.

STEP 5—COMPARISON WITH SIMILAR IDEAS OR PHENOMENA
WHERE YOU SEE THE RED ELEPHANT, YOU ALWAYS FIND
DEPENDABLE LUMBER.

STEP 7—ACTION OR PROGNOSTICATION STATEMENT
CALL THE LUMBER NUMBER, WITH A 384 AND A 2222.

Example 3, Steps 1, 2, 3, 4, 7 (for radio)

STEP 1—INITIAL STATEMENT
OUR BIGGEST SALE OF THE YEAR!

STEP 2—REINFORCEMENT-REPETITION
OUR ONE AND ONLY.

STEP 3—DETAILS AND EXAMPLES
A TEN-PIECE COOK SET, USUALLY $79.95, NOW JUST $69.88. SAVE ON
JOHNSON DINNERWARE BY THE PLACE SETTING OR IN 45-PIECE SETS.

STEP 4—ASSIGNING ORIGIN OR CAUSE
FOUNDER'S DAY! OUR BIGGEST SALE OF THE YEAR.

STEP 7—ACTION OR PROGNOSTICATION STATEMENT
FOUNDER'S DAY! MAY 5TH, AT BENTLEY'S.

Here is how the copy looks to the announcer:

OUR BIGGEST SALE OF THE YEAR! OUR ONE AND ONLY. A TEN-PIECE
COOK SET, USUALLY $79.95, NOW JUST $69.88. SAVE ON JOHNSON
DINNERWARE BY THE PLACE SETTING OR IN 45-PIECE SETS.
FOUNDER'S DAY! MAY 5TH, AT BENTLEY'S.

Example 4, Steps 1, 2, 3, 7 (for radio)

STEP 1—INITIAL STATEMENT

NOW'S THE TIME TO GET STARTED CHICKS WHILE LOW SUMMER
PRICES ARE IN EFFECT AT WATSON'S HATCHERY.

STEP 2—REINFORCEMENT-REPETITION

SEVERAL THOUSAND STARTED CHICKS, THREE TO FIVE WEEKS OLD,
ARE NOW READY FOR IMMEDIATE DELIVERY.

STEP 3—DETAILS AND EXAMPLES

AUSTRA-WHITES, HAMP-WHITES, AND WHITE-LEGHORNS, ALL FROM
BLOOD-TESTED FLOCKS. BOTH PULLETS AND STRAIGHT RUNS
AVAILABLE.

STEP 7—ACTION OR PROGNOSTICATION STATEMENT

ORDER NOW OR PICK UP STARTED CHICKS FROM WATSON'S
HATCHERY, 1400 WEST SIXTH, TOWNVILLE.

Here is how the copy looked to the announcer:

NOW'S THE TIME TO GET STARTED CHICKS WHILE LOW SUMMER
PRICES ARE IN EFFECT AT WATSON'S HATCHERY. SEVERAL THOUSAND
STARTED CHICKS, THREE TO FIVE WEEKS OLD, ARE NOW READY FOR
IMMEDIATE DELIVERY. AUSTRA-WHITES, HAMP-WHITES, AND
WHITE-LEGHORNS, ALL FROM BLOOD-TESTED FLOCKS. BOTH PULLETS
AND STRAIGHT RUNS AVAILABLE. ORDER NOW OR PICK UP STARTED
CHICKS FROM WATSON'S HATCHERY, 1400 WEST SIXTH, TOWNVILLE.

Example 5, Steps 1, 2, 3, 5, 7 (for television)

VIDEO	AUDIO
STEP 1—INITIAL STATEMENT	
CAR ALONE IN FIELD.	ANNCR: A CAR IS JUST A CAR UNTIL SOMEONE STANDS BEHIND IT.
STEP 2—REINFORCEMENT-REPETITION STATEMENT	
AT COURTESY, WE DO JUST THAT.	
STEP 3—DETAILS OR EXAMPLES	
POP ON SALESPERSON NEXT TO CAR.	OUR SALES PROFESSIONALS HELP CHOOSE THE CAR THAT'S RIGHT FOR YOU.

POP ON OFFICE GIRL.	AN EFFICIENT OFFICE STAFF COMPLETES THE NECESSARY PAPERWORK.
POP ON FINANCE PERSONNEL	AND AFFORDABLE FINANCING IS AVAILABLE THROUGH OUR CREATIVE FINANCING EXECUTIVES.
POP ON VIP	TOP MANAGEMENT IS READILY AVAILABLE TO MAKE SURE YOU GET A GOOD BUY.
POP ON SERVICE REP.	AND WE'VE GOT MR. GOODWRENCH STANDING BEHIND YOUR CAR SHOULD YOU NEED PROPER SERVICING.

STEP 5—COMPARISON WITH SIMILAR IDEAS OF PHENOMENA

WHOLE GROUP POPS.	SO POP INTO COURTESY, BECAUSE CARS ARE ONLY AS GOOD AS THE PEOPLE WHO STAND BEHIND THEM.

STEP 7—ACTION OR PROGNOSTICATION

	AND OUR PEOPLE ARE GOOD!
VIDIFONT: COURTESY CARS, ADDRESS.[10]	

Example 6, Steps 1, 2, 3, 4, 7 (for television)

VIDEO	AUDIO

STEP 1—INITIAL STATEMENT

MEDIUM SHOT OF LA-Z-BOY CHAIR.	VOICE: FOR TOTAL COMFORT, MOST PEOPLE THINK A LA-Z-BOY CHAIR IS ONE OF A KIND.

STEP 2—REINFORCEMENT-REPETITION

	BUT WATCH THIS, AND THINK AGAIN.

STEP 3—DETAILS OR EXAMPLES

A LA-Z-BOY CHAIR BEGINS WHIRLING RAPIDLY TOWARD VIEWER THROUGH A TUNNEL OF FABRICS.	

10. Courtesy Duane Francescht, President, Financial Marketing Concepts, Tallahassee, Florida.

STEP 4—ASSIGNING ORIGIN OR CAUSE

SHOT OF MULTI-FABRICS.   YES, THINK OF A SELECTION OF OVER
                                                500 FABRICS AND 126 DIFFERENT
                                                STYLES, AND YOU'LL NEVER THINK OF
                                                LA-Z-BOY AS ONE OF A KIND AGAIN.

STEP 7—ACTION OR PROGNOSTICATION STATEMENT

SHOT OF SEVERAL LA-Z-BOY CHAIRS.   THE LA-Z-BOY CHAIR COMPANY. WE
                                                DELIVER COMFORT THAT FITS YOUR
                                                STYLE.[11]

ASSIGNMENTS: THE MODIFIED SEVEN-STEP COMMERCIAL

Repetitious routines are the surest way to learn how to write. The following assignments are suggestions for beginning.

1. Write two kinds of 30-second radio-television commercials using Steps 1, 2, 3, 4, 5, 7.

2. Write two kinds of 20-second radio-television commercials using Steps 1, 2, 3, 7.

3. Write two kinds of 10-second radio-television commercials using Steps 1, 2, 7.

4. Write two kinds of radio-television commercials using Steps 1, 2, 4, 7. You select length.

5. Write two kinds of 20-second television commercials using Steps 1, 2, 3, 5, 6, 7.

6. Write several 30-second television commercials using the steps necessary to develop each one.

---

11. Courtesy LA-Z-BOY, John J. Chase, Director of Advertising, Monroe, Michigan.

CHAPTER **6**

The Dramatic Commercial

Before you begin writing the dramatic commercial, you should be proficient in using the six-step and seven-step processes. Mastering these increases your ability to communicate in all kinds of writing.

Professionally, the Dramatic commercial is used because it involves human beings in conflict with themselves, others, or the environment. The preparation for using the five-step process as a writing technique is the same as that for the six- and seven-step processes. Detailed information is essential. Not until all data preparation is complete can an adequate thesis, theme, or central idea be developed and related through the product or service to a human problem, need, feeling, or desire.

STORY DEVELOPMENT

Once the data preparation is complete, the copywriter is ready to begin searching for a story as an illustration. The central idea of a Sanka commercial implies, in terms of a human problem, why drink something that disrupts your well-being? If drinking coffee upsets you, it is the wrong drink. Drink decaffeinated instead. Developing a story to illustrate this thesis, theme, or central idea as it relates to a problem, need, feeling, or desire is called *plotting*.

Plotting

What is a *plot?* For the copywriter, it is the outline of a story to be told to illustrate a human problem. There are many explanations of how to develop a plot, but most teachers agree that the easiest way to understand what a plot is and how to develop one is to think of a plot as an organized plan for a story. As such, it basically consists of a goal desired by the leading character and the problems the character runs into in achieving or not achieving that goal.

Keep in mind that a plot, the skeleton story, may be simple or complex in structure. A simple plot is generally reduced to a single statement of the goal to be achieved by the leading character. In commercial copywriting the solution is always achieved: "My headache is completely gone."

Plots differ in various ways. They differ as much as does the body structure of human beings. The essential fact about a plot for a commercial is that a writer with a thesis, theme, or central idea related to a human problem, need, feeling, or desire must devise a story plan that brings the central concept, the plot, and the product or service together. In this way the central idea and the plot and the service become inextricably linked.

Because the plot is the story line, always keep in mind that it will be listened to in direct ratio to the interest created by its ability to solve a problem. In other words, the commercial will be interesting in terms of its conflict(s), the ups and downs encountered by the leading character, and the way or manner in which the conflict(s) is solved.

A problem in plotting for a commercial is that the writer's story time may be limited to 30, 20, or even 10 seconds. That means there is little time to create a conflict and solve it.

One of the more helpful ways of learning how to develop a plot for a commercial is to study the techniques used by established commercial writers. As you watch commercials, be sure to note the name of the product or service and how it is interrelated with a basic human problem, need, feeling, or desire and the thesis, theme, or central idea. Also note that the product or service frequently is the good-guy overcoming the villain, the basic problem, which may be as simple as an inadequate way of doing something. In other words, the use of the product corrects or does away with the problem that has become a conflict in the life of the character in the commercial's story.

Finally, plotting is listing the sequence of events, stating what is to happen or take place in the story.

Selecting a Character

There are many ways to create a character for a commercial. Creatively, these two aspects of storytelling, plotting and characterization, may or may not occur to the writer at the same time. Sometimes the story comes to the writer after the characters have been conceived; sometimes the story comes first. When the commercial's story comes first, the writer must create or develop characters to fit the story. The product or service basically determines both the plot and the characters.

Single-purpose plots are easier for the listener-viewer to comprehend. Regardless of the length of the commercial, the leading character must always be directly concerned with a specific problem, need, feeling, or desire. This specific concern helps the listener-viewer *empathize* with the character. This empathic correlation between the character's problem in the commercial and the listener-viewer's real or imagined need, feeling, or desire determines whether the product or service will be purchased and used.

To help you create an interesting character, which in commercials is a human being doing something in a normal, human way, remember the frame of reference principle. Your leading character must be a person with whom the listener-viewer can readily identify. *A leading commercial character should never be a neurotic indulging in his or her favorite form of neurosis.*

Developing a Characterization

There are two specific ways to give life to a character for a commercial: *objective characterization* and *subjective characterization.*

Objective Characterization   In real-life situations most people are seen objectively and are judged by how they seem to be rather than by what and how they actually are. These judgments are based on how others see a person. What is seen includes size, build, and appearance, and how the person moves, dresses, and responds. These observations give the listener-viewer objective clues about the person's character.

Subjective Characterization   Subjective character development reveals the individual's standards of conduct, thought processes, emotions, imagination, view of life, and whether the character thinks like an introvert or an extrovert. Subjective characterization is concerned with the inner person. This includes the character's mental and emotional accomplishments as well as how the character thinks and feels about everything including *self*.

Regardless of the method used in creating a character, a commercial copywriter must make the leading person in the commercial likable or even lovable. The character may be an angel, a devil, or anything in between, but the emotions the character arouses in the listener-viewer must cause admiration, amusement, or sympathy. Always, of course, the product or service must be involved.

On occasion the plot may call for a person who is not likable and although the listener-viewer is not usually interested in a character that cannot be admired, such a figure may be used as a device. This means that the character is always overcome or outdone by the product or service. In this way the listener-viewer identifies with the product or service because it overcame the "bad guy".

Creating and Developing Conflict

Every commercial must open with a conflict in its character's interest, purpose, or intent. This opening is especially needed in the dramatic commercial because the essence of dramatic action is conflict.

In many television movies, conflict in the plot consists of the good guy against the bad guy. But conflict may occur within the person, as in *Dr. Jekyll and Mr. Hyde*. Or conflict may be as intricate and as personal as in Shakespeare's *Hamlet*. Conflict may be man or woman against the elements, as in *The Swiss Family Robinson* or current expeditions into outer space with *Superman*. Conflict may consist of a man against the leaders of society, such as in *Robin Hood* or in a master-spy plot.

In commercial writing, the most successful conflict is that of a person having problems with self (aches, pains, itches, tastes, looks, etc.). Man against man, man against woman, or woman against woman are all interesting conflicts used in writing commercials. When the conflict is a broad one, such as a person against the elements (rain, snow, hail, sleet, cold, or heat), the elements are frequently assisted by a villain or a hero.

The purpose of a conflict, in the guise of a menace, opposition, or person, may also determine the plot you need in planning a commercial. The chief task of the menace, or opposition, is to present an obstacle during the rising action. Such statements as "I drink real coffee" are obstacles that your character must overcome, or must be helped to overcome. The use of these devices is determined by the length and the nature of the commercial.

Conflict and the Commercial

The intensity of a conflicting force in a commercial is usually determined by the product or service. For example, in a Sanka Coffee commercial, the conflict is between the individual who likes "real coffee" and the notion that "too much caffeine makes me nervous." Caffeine prevents his playing better golf. This he dislikes. That is a conflict.

There is no room for physical action in this conflict. But there is conflict through the intensity he experiences. The amount may not be world-shaking, but it is psychologically sound and therefore interesting to the listener-viewer who may be bothered by the same problem. When the character is helped to win out against such a problem, the listener-viewer tends to believe that he or she can win too.

As a copywriter, you should have little trouble discovering or inventing conflicts that are adequate for a commercial because life is full of such obstacles. They are everywhere and are a natural part of life. That is why television commercials are developed around them. Kids dislike a breakfast cereal because it "is good for them." You work hard, but your floors or windows still do not "shine." "I love the rich flavor. It's the caffeine I can do without" and "ring around the collar" are favorite conflicts.

Conflicts are without doubt the reason that life and living are almost always a problem. For example, every individual who is unable or afraid to make a decision is, at that moment, facing a conflict. Not being able to make a decision psychologically means that the individual is facing a crisis. Actually, life would be very dull without these moments. Similarly, a commercial without an obstacle or without a conflict becomes dull. Commercials without conflicts are not worth the listener-viewer's time, nor the cost of production.

Developing Dramatic Action

Every commercial, whether it follows a six-step, seven-step, or dramatic five-step process, must have, or must be given, the element known as *dramatic action*. Saying that a commercial must have dramatic action is just another way of saying that conflict or struggle must be present or implied in each commercial. Therefore, it naturally follows that the more difficult the opposition or obstacle to be overcome during the rising action, the more intently the listener-viewer will view the commercial. This is true because the greater the challenge to the leading character, the more the listener-viewer is likely to empathize with his or her effort to overcome the problem.

If the leading character of a commercial is to seem "admirable," worthy of empathy, he or she must not be limited to overcoming a minor obstacle. For example, dramatic action (obstacle and conflict) is used in overcoming the problem of knowing when a brown towel or dark garment can be said to be clean. The opening of the Gain detergent commercial introduces the leading character (a male in a shower) and gives him immediate action, that of tossing a brown towel out to his wife. The action introduces the conflict that is to be solved. How do you know when a dark-colored towel is clean? Both sight and smell are introduced immediately. You cannot see if a dark towel is clean, but you can *smell* the cleanliness after it has been washed in Gain.

Seeing a character meet and overcome an obstacle makes the commercial worth the time spent watching it. That the commercial is worth watching is the reason this aspect of plot development, dramatic action, is needed whether the commercial is concerned with ideas, emotions, human foibles, machinery, or computers.

In summary, to develop dramatic action in a commercial you must put the leading character in a situation that involves conflict. While you are solving the problem, be sure to use as much appeal to the senses as possible, especially sensory appeals to sight, sound, smell, and touch. Taste is extremely important in some commercials. Notice how important taste and sight become in the commercials about the orange juice that "isn't just for breakfast anymore."

Having a Goal for the Leading Character

After the main character of your commercial has been conceived, you should then relate the character to a goal. (This is pointed out in the discussion on *rising action*.) The goal may be external, such as getting rid of dandruff, or internal, such as getting rid of bad breath or an arthritic pain. Whatever the problem, it must be solved by the story line in your commercial. This is important because it helps capture the listener-viewer's attention and convince him or her to "go and do likewise."

One way to develop a goal is to have adequate conflicts or obstacles. Remember, if your character does not have a problem in the beginning of the commercial, there is obviously no basic *plot question* to be solved. Without a plot question to solve, no interest will develop. Remember too that if the plot question (how is the problem to be solved and the goal achieved) is answered too soon or too easily, interest in the plot will be weak. In other words, the goal must always *seem* difficult to achieve.

In any well-plotted and well-written commercial, the action never progresses in a single straight line of known advances toward the outcome. Unforeseen conflict increases the listener-viewer's interest in whether the character will succeed. If there is no doubt that the person will find an answer to the plot question and will achieve his or her goal without struggle, interest in the leading character and the product or service is weakened and frequently lost. To avoid this loss of interest, the action taken in achieving the goal must be a determined action, an act of will. This decision making by the leading character makes the commercial worth watching.

Creating Rising Action and a Climax

The copywriter must be sure to give the leading character in the commercial a desire to win. "The doctor says too much caffeine makes me nervous." In that statement the desire to "win" is understood. Another example is the conflict between the leading character saying "Parkay" and the Parkay package saying "butter." The desire to win by having the last word is used in this commercial to catch and hold the listener-viewer's attention.

The writer can strengthen the leading character's desire to win by starting the opening scene on a low key. By beginning on a low level of excitement, the dramatic action has a chance to rise as the struggle progresses. Always avoid starting a dramatic sequence at too high a level of intensity. When you do, there is likely to be no way the dramatic action can increase adequately. And a rise in the dramatic action is essential if a climax is to be achieved.

Naturally, each action must run its course against an obstacle before being solved. This delay can be done by having the character face additional conflicts. The best way to keep conflict working is to have it meet a more difficult conflict. Just when a solution seems possible, the leading character is faced with a new problem greater than the last.

To illustrate the concept of rising action that leads to a climax, let us compare it to climbing a ladder. Each step takes the climber closer to the top. But while he is going up the ladder, the climber slips and slides off each rung. This slipping, sliding, and nearly falling back to the ground, yet continuing to climb, is equivalent to meeting and overcoming a series of conflicts.

Near the top of the ladder, at the climax, the climber will find the answer to the plot's question, Why climb the ladder? The answer is that you can see farther standing at the top than you can on the ground.

One of the most helpful ways of developing a well-planned rising action in a commercial is to have a *cause* that is responsible for the main character's problems. For example, bad breath is the cause that keeps the leading character from having friends. If the leading character wants to acquire friends, the cause for not having them must be removed. When the cause is removed through a series of rising actions, the leading character will have achieved a climax, a desired *effect*.

The technique of *cause to effect* can be used to develop rising action in all commercials. Just remember that the cause must be overcome before a result, and the desired effect, can be achieved.

One caution about using cause and effect. An accidental occurrence cannot be used to triumph over a cause. Accidents just happen. As an unplanned incident, the accident may be interesting, but according to all the rules of dramatic writing, it is called an act of God. The character has no choice in the matter and therefore cannot exercise control over the results.

It is true that accidents and coincidences happen all the time in real life, just as chance is an important part of our daily living and is accepted by us. Thousands and thousands of peoples' lives are shaped and reshaped by coincidence and accidents. But when a coincidence or accident is used in a commercial to solve a human problem, there is no *cause to effect* to make the results that occur the product of logic and reasoning. When a reasonable choice is not made by the character, the listener-viewer is inclined to disbelieve the situation and lose/interest in the product or service.

Making Cause to Effect Reasonable

The basic rule to remember about plot construction for a commercial is this: *Never* have a turning point take place unexpectedly or coincidentally. A copywriter can use coincidence as an element of plot construction, however, if the fact that it is to occur has been mentioned or implied earlier.

Throughout the history of commercial writing all conflicts and obstacles are more believable when introduced by:

1. Establishing action that is related to the mood of the commercial. Note the openings in most of the coffee commercials.

2. Having someone make a statement that the leading character cannot possibly accomplish a given effect and then having him do it. Many beer commercials use this technique.

3. Having a character introduce a problem that seems impossible to solve and then solving it. Many commercials do this. The brown towel Gain commercial is an example.

4. Using a device, such as a letter, a telephone, a message, or a tape recording.

Cause to Effect in the Creation of Personality

Another problem the copywriter faces in the use of *cause to effect* is the need to keep the specific personality of each character from taking on contrary traits. The writer can avoid this problem by keeping in mind that a person rarely acts contrary to his or her basic nature unless forced to do so. When a copywriter has a character do something that is contrary to his or her dominant personality characteristic, the action will be unconvincing unless sufficient alternatives have been established to allow the character this choice. For example, the person who drank coffee was tense when playing golf. After switching to "real coffee" Sanka, he was able to relax and enjoy the game, even though he played no better.

Every copywriter should also keep in mind that characters do not fight and die for abstractions any more convincingly than do living people. For the most part, people struggle for particular and specific things. Every conflicting event or action must be full of specific details that help or hinder the character's advance toward a goal. Specific details help the listener-viewer feel the goal that the character is struggling to achieve. An example in one commercial is that of having dentures become "a real part of your mouth" because the person speaking selected and is using a particular denture adhesive.

Obviously the problems that get in the way of achieving a goal for which the character is struggling are not mentioned unless someone in your commercial asks about it. It is also much better writing technique when your thesis, theme, or central idea is kept in the background and is *sensed*, or *felt*, by your character. For example, "Have a clean brown towel, Mr.?"

The writing is also stronger when a desire to achieve is sensed by the listener-viewer to be present in the character's personality. This way it will be empathized with as the character struggles against the problem that seems to prevent achievement of the goal.

Concluding the Dramatic Commercial

Whatever the subject matter, a dramatic commercial must have a resolution, a finish, an end, a *denouement*. At the end of every commercial the problem or problems the leading character is having must be solved so that the individual can be seen "living happily ever after." "My game hasn't improved, but I'm doing just great since I switched to Sanka brand coffee."

Summary

Every commercial plot must indicate that a character is facing a problem. This problem must be solved through the character's efforts. The effort must involve the product or service and may be as simple as switching to a different product. The solution must be near the end of the commercial. The product or service is therefore reemphasized as a solution to the character's problem.

BASIC STYLES OF DRAMATIC COMMERCIALS

Dramatic commercials may be divided into several styles. Practical writers of the episodic and miniplay commercial tend to stick with two basic classifications: *romantic* and *realistic*.

Of course the dramatic commercial can be mixed with all the other kinds of commercials. But, generally speaking, romantic subjects are about self-concepts, or fantasies. Romanticism is life as the listener-viewer would like to live it.

The exact opposite of romanticism is realism. Realistic subjects are about the daily facts of life as it exists in a particular environment. "Check out all the low, low prices at Dubey's! I did!"

The romantic commercial is by far the more popular because most people listen and view in an effort to escape reality. They watch television commercials to help fulfill their wishes and desires vicariously. For some, watching commercials is a form of shopping. It is a way of finding something new to add interest to the individual's lifestyle.

Some critics look upon fantasy and romanticism as synonymous. Others believe it is the responsibility of the copywriter to turn reality into romanticism. The quotation above, "Check out all the low, low prices at Dubey 's! I did!" is a romantic treatment of reality in that commercial. It is not fantasy.

The dramatic commercial copywriter must also be aware at all times that when the listener-viewer can figure out what is going to happen ahead of time, the commercial lacks the dramatic qualities it needs to hold attention. When the commercial fails to hold attention, the listener-viewer is likely to begin feeling there are more desirable ways of spending time. Commercial writing is at its best when the listener-viewer is willing to hear a commercial again and again.

HOW TO WRITE THE DRAMATIC COMMERCIAL: THE FIVE-STEP PROCESS

Now that you are familiar with the general procedures in developing a dramatic commercial, the five-step process will take you from beginning to end of the commercial. Even a straight narrative commercial can be made more interesting by using the five-step process.

As you go through the five-step procedure unit by unit, note the ever present need for an implied thesis, theme, or central idea as it relates to a problem, need, feeling, or desire.

Step 1—Situation and Characterization

In the opening seconds of a dramatic commercial the leading character(s) must come face to face with a thesis, theme, or central idea as it relates to a problem, need, feeling, or desire. Naturally the character needs, or wants, to solve this conflict. Sometimes the character is asked by a second person to meet a situation or problem and solve it. For example, "Does you husband notice clean clothes?" "Does your husband prefer potatoes or dressing for dinner?"

The copywriter must be sure that the central idea, the problem, and the situation are interrelated. Moreover, this interrelationship must be correlated in such a way that the listener-viewer's attention is caught immediately. Here is an opening. Note how the thesis, theme, or central idea and a problem are presented by implication.

STEP 1—SITUATION AND CHARACTERIZATION

| TWO MEN ARE PRACTICE PUTTING. | FIRST MALE: AH-UH-AH! MISSED AGAIN! |
| | SECOND MALE: JIM! IT'S ONLY PRACTICE! |

Step 2—Rising Action

After this opening in which the commercial presents a character and a situation in which he is obviously facing a conflict (problem, need, feeling, or desire), the copywriter introduces an additional conflict that must be faced by the leading character. Each conflict is a problem about which the character needs to make a decision. These succeeding conflicts are all related to the initial conflict. Together they constitute the rising action in the commercial's story line. Each new conflict or problem in the rising action becomes a bit more difficult for the character to manage or overcome. Because of the difficulty the character is having solving the problem, increased effort is necessary, and additional doubt is created in the listener-viewer as to whether the character will be able to cope with the problem. Here is an example of how Step 2 is presented. Note how the thesis, theme, central idea in relation to a problem, need, feeling, or desire is made clear to the listener-viewer.

STEP 2—RISING ACTION

ENTERING CLUBHOUSE.	FIRST MALE: I'VE HAD TOO MUCH CAFFEINE LATELY. DOCTOR SAYS IT MAKES ME NERVOUS.
	SECOND MALE: WELL, DON'T YOU DRINK SANKA BRAND DECAFFEINATED COFFEE?
	FIRST MALE: I DRINK REAL COFFEE.

Step 3—The Climax

Now we're beginning to get the full picture of the character's problem. Caffeine makes him nervous. He plays lousy golf. And yet he insists on drinking coffee that seems to make it impossible for him to play better.

Additional rising action, conflicts, may be introduced at this time if the length of the commercial, the amount of air time, permits. The purpose of these conflicts in the rising action are to create doubt as to whether the character will win over his problem in the final action, the climax. Always, by the time the story reaches the climax, the leading character is called upon to give his or her best effort to triumph over the problem. In other words, the climax occurs when the leading character seems capable of overcoming and demonstrates an ability to overcome the major obstacle that stands in the way of achievement. Here is an example in the same commercial.

STEP 3—THE CLIMAX

> SECOND MALE: SANKA BRAND IS REAL
> COFFEE. HERE, TRY SOME.
> FIRST MALE: (DOUBTFUL AT FIRST,
> THEN HE TASTES IT AND . . .)
> UMMM. THIS IS GOOD COFFEE.

Step 4—Falling Action

Up to and during the climactic action the listener-viewer is not quite sure the leading character will solve the problem. Even after the climax, there is no certainty the solution will turn out for the better. How the solution to the problem really evolves comes after the climax. The unit in which this occurs is referred to as *falling action*. This section of the five-step process includes those activities and events that are essential to an efficient and effective conclusion of the commercial's story line. Sometimes this falling action is just one event in a commercial, an event that in turn leads to the end of the story, referred to as the *denouement*. Here is an example of falling action.

STEP 4—FALLING ACTION

TWO MALES BACK ON THE PRACTICE GREEN, PUTTING.

FIRST MALE: AH-UH-AH! MISSED AGAIN! MY GAME'S NOT A LOT BETTER, BUT I AM SINCE I SWUNG OVER TO SANKA BRAND.
SECOND MALE: (CHUCKLES, AGREEING.)

Step 5—Denouement

This is the final action in every dramatic commercial's story line. The denouement is literally the conclusion, the final scene in the commercial.

Its purpose is to demonstrate and illustrate how the leading character is finally affected after triumphing over the obstacle that initially got in the way of his or her success. The denouement is the final statement of what is to happen to the leading character. What happens is usually an implication of what can happen to the listener-viewer if he or she has the same problem and will use the same product or service. Here is an example of the denouement in this same commercial.

STEP 5—DENOUEMENT

LATER, IN THE CLUBHOUSE.	SECOND MALE: (CHUCKLING AS HE SEES FIRST MALE ENJOYING HIMSELF AND NO LONGER
VIEW OF PRODUCT.	TENSE.) SANKA BRAND! ENJOY YOUR COFFEE AND ENJOY YOURSELF.

Here is the full script of the Sanka commercial. Because we are concerned with writing, emphasis is on the audio.

VIDEO	AUDIO
TWO MALES ON PRACTICE PUTTING GREEN.	FIRST MALE: AH-UH-AH! MISSED AGAIN!
	SECOND MALE: JIM, IT'S ONLY PRACTICE!
ENTERING CLUBHOUSE.	FIRST MALE: I'VE HAD TOO MUCH CAFFEINE LATELY. DOCTOR SAYS IT MAKES ME NERVOUS.
	SECOND MALE: WELL, DON'T YOU DRINK SANKA BRAND DECAFFEINATED COFFEE?
	FIRST MALE: I DRINK REAL COFFEE.
	SECOND MALE: SANKA BRAND IS REAL COFFEE. HERE, TRY SOME.
	FIRST MALE: (DOUBTFUL AT FIRST, THEN HE TASTES IT AND . . .) UM-M-M. THIS IS GOOD COFFEE.
	SECOND MALE: (CHUCKLES, AGREEING)
TWO MALES BACK ON THE PRACTICE GREEN, PUTTING.	FIRST MALE: AH-UH-AH! MISSED AGAIN! MY GAMES NOT A LOT BETTER, BUT I AM SINCE I SWUNG OVER TO SANKA BRAND.

The Dramatic Commercial   107

LATER, IN THE CLUBHOUSE.

SECOND MALE: (CHUCKLING AS HE
SEES FIRST MALE ENJOYING
HIMSELF AND NO LONGER
TENSE.) SANKA BRAND! ENJOY
YOUR COFFEE AND ENJOY
YOURSELF!

Examples of the Five-Step Dramatic Commercial

Here are examples of the five-step process dramatic commercial. Each example will help you visualize how the dramatic commercial goes together step by step. Only a suggestion of the video is included because emphasis is on writing rather than production. As you study each commercial, pick out the thesis, theme, or central idea and note how it relates to a problem, need, feeling, or desire.

Example 1

VIDEO	AUDIO

STEP 1—SITUATION AND CHARACTERIZATION

MRS. TALBOT, SITTING BEHIND TABLE, OBVIOUSLY HAS A HEADACHE. FOUR WHITE RECTANGULAR BOXES STANDING IN A ROW. ANNOUNCER AT END OF TABLE.	ANNCR. BET YOU THINK THESE PAIN RELIEVERS ARE ALL ALIKE, MRS. TALBOT? MRS. TALBOT: SURE DO.

STEP 2—RISING ACTION

	ANNCR: LET'S SEE. (TURNS FIRST BOX TO REVEAL NUMBER.) TWO REGULAR TABLETS . . . 650 MILLIGRAMS. THESE OTHER PAIN RELIEVERS ALSO 650 MILLIGRAMS. (TURNS ANOTHER BOX.) SIX HUNDRED FIFTY MILLIGRAMS. STILL THINK THEY'RE ALL THE SAME? MRS. TALBOT: YUP!

STEP 3—CLIMAX

	ANNCR: LOOK HERE. (TURNS FOURTH BOX TO REVEAL NUMBER.) EIGHT HUNDRED MILLIGRAMS!

MRS. TALBOT: ANACIN! I DIDN'T KNOW ANACIN HAD MORE PAIN RELIEVER!

STEP 4—FALLING ACTION

ANNCR: YES, MORE PAIN RELIEVER AND A SPECIAL COMBINATION OF MEDICAL INGREDIENTS. THAT'S THE ANACIN DIFFERENCE. SO NOW WHICH PAIN RELIEVER?

STEP 5—DENOUEMENT

CAMERA ON PRODUCT.

MRS. TALBOT: ANACIN!
ANNCR: (VO) GET THE ANACIN DIFFERENCE.[1]

Example 2

Some commercials have music as a background. Other commercials have music as a theme, a technique by which the sponsor or the product or service is identified. These logo-type musical signatures are generally used in the beginning of the commercial and again during the close. The musical, or singing, logo, has been used for years. It is a very popular form of sponsor, product, or service identification. Singing logos are successful primarily because people enjoy singing along with them, or humming the music. The logo music becomes a familiar tune to be remembered and enjoyed.

The following dramatic commercial uses visual identification in the beginning and a singing-logo identification in its conclusion.

VIDEO	AUDIO

STEP 1—SITUATION AND CHARACTERIZATION

MUSIC UNDER AS TRUCK PULLS INTO HARDEE'S® RESTAURANT PARKING LOT. YOUNG MALE ENTERS AND GOES TO COUNTER. HE OBVIOUSLY WANTS FOOD, BUT IS ALSO INTERESTED IN FEMALES. WAITRESS STOPS TO SERVE HIM.	RUNNER: DO I SMELL BISCUITS BAKING? BARB: WOULD YOU LIKE TO SEE THEM? (SHOWS HIM A PAN OF BISCUITS.) RUNNER: M-M-M-M-. . . . YOU BAKE THESE UP FRESH EVERY MORNING? BARB: FRESH EVERY MORNING.

1. Courtesy Steven Gootzeit, Group Product Manager, Whitehall Laboratories. Commercial produced by John F. Murray Advertising Agency, New York, New York. © 1980 Whitehall Laboratories.

STEP 2—RISING ACTION

RUNNER: HOMEMADE BISCUITS. SURE
DOES BEAT WHAT I'VE BEEN
HAVING.
BARB: WHAT WOULD YOU LIKE?
COUNTRY HAM, SAUSAGE,
CHOPPED BEEFSTEAK?
RUNNER: GIVE ME A STEAK NOW AND
WRAP ME UP A SAUSAGE.

STEP 3—CLIMAX
GIVING HIM PACKAGES.

BARB: OK . . . TWO HOT BREAKFAST
BISCUITS, JUICE AND COFFEE. . . .
ANYTHING ELSE?

STEP 4—FALLING ACTION

RUNNER: ONE THING. MARRY ME?

STEP 5—DENOUEMENT
MUSIC: HARDEE'S LOGO SONG.

"HARDEE'S BEST EATIN' IN TOWN, UP
AND DOWN AND ALL AROUND."[2]

Example 3

Sometimes a five-step dramatic commercial may be combined with other
process types. The following example combines a singing logo and a voice
representing the product or service. Therefore this Southern Bell "Father"
commercial may be diagramed two ways. First it is diagramed as a five-step
process. The theme can be stated as "call those you love by long distance."

VIDEO   AUDIO

STEP 1—SITUATION AND CHARACTERIZATION
SINGING LOGO.

"REACH OUT, REACH OUT AND TOUCH
SOMEONE."

STEP 2—RISING ACTION

ANNCR: (VO) KEEPING WITHIN YOUR
BUDGET IS TOUGHER THESE DAYS.
SO IT'S GOOD TO KNOW WHEN
THERE'S A BARGAIN AROUND.

2. Courtesy Connie L. Logan, Manager, Advertising Hardee's Food Systems. Used by
Permission. Commercial produced by Benton and Bowles, New York, © 1979 Hardee's Food
System, Inc.

Hardee's

"MARRY ME"

Length: 30 Seconds
Comm'l No.: QHAE 9309

(MUSIC UNDER AS TRUCK PULLS IN)

RUNNER: Do I smell biscuits baking?

BARB: Would you like to see them?

RUNNER: Mmm...You bake these up fresh every morning?

BARB: Fresh every morning.

RUNNER: Homemade biscuits. Sure does beat what I've been having.

BARB: What would you like?

Country ham, sausage, chopped beef-steak?

RUNNER: Give me a steak now and wrap me up a sausage.

BARB: OK...Two hot breakfast biscuits, juice and coffee...Anything else?

RUNNER: One thing. Marry me?

SONG: Hardee's! Best eatin' in town, up and down and all around.

Courtesy Benton and Bowles

The Dramatic Commercial   111

STEP 3—CLIMAX

ANSWERING TELEPHONE.	DAUGHTER: HELLO.
TALKING INTO TELEPHONE.	FATHER; HOW'S MY LITTLE GIRL IN SAN DIEGO?
	DAUGHTER: DADDY! I CAN SET MY WATCH BY YOU. AH-H-H, FIVE O'CLOCK BACK THERE. LONG DISTANCE RATES JUST WENT ON. WE'LL TALK EXACTLY TEN MINUTES, AND IT'LL COST YOU FOUR DOLLARS, RIGHT?
	FATHER; ONLY TWO DOLLARS AND FIFTY-SEVEN CENTS, DIANE.

STEP 4—FALLING ACTION

	ANNCR: (VO) REACH OUT WITH LONG DISTANCE. IT'S A LOT OF LOVE FOR THE MONEY.

STEP 5—DENOUEMENT

	DAUGHTER: YOU KNOW ALL THE BARGAINS, DADDY.

Note: You may also diagram this commercial as a modified seven-step process with a five-step unit interjected. This combination diagram might be as follows.

VIDEO	AUDIO

STEP 1—(SEVEN-STEP) INITIAL STATEMENT

SINGING LOGO.	"REACH OUT, REACH OUT AND TOUCH SOMEONE."

STEP 2—(SEVEN-STEP) REINFORCEMENT-REPETITION STATEMENT

	ANNCR: (VO) KEEPING WITHIN YOUR BUDGET IS TOUGHER THESE DAYS. SO IT'S GOOD TO KNOW WHEN THERE'S A BARGAIN AROUND.

STEP 3—(SEVEN-STEP) DETAILS OR EXAMPLES
   (*FIVE-STEP, STEP 1—SITUATION AND CHARACTERIZATION*)

ANSWERING PHONE.	DAUGHTER: HELLO.
TALKING INTO TELEPHONE.	FATHER: HOW'S MY LITTLE GIRL IN SAN DIEGO?

DAUGHTER: DADDY! I CAN SET MY
WATCH BY YOU. AH-H-H, FIVE
O'CLOCK BACK THERE. LONG
DISTANCE RATES JUST WENT ON.
WE'LL TALK EXACTLY TEN
MINUTES AND IT'LL COST YOU
FOUR DOLLARS, RIGHT?

(*FIVE-STEP,* *STEP 3—CLIMAX*)

FATHER: ONLY TWO DOLLARS AND
FIFTY-SEVEN CENTS, DIANE.

STEP 5—(SEVEN-STEP) COMPARISON WITH SIMILAR IDEAS

ANNCR: (VO) REACH OUT WITH LONG
DISTANCE. IT'S A LOT OF LOVE
FOR THE MONEY.

STEP 7—(SEVEN-STEP) STATING OR PROGNOSTICATING RESULTS:
(*FIVE-STEP,* *STEPS 4 AND 5—FALLING ACTION AND DENOUEMENT*)

DAUGHTER: YOU KNOW ALL THE
BARGAINS DADDY.[3]

Example 4

Sometimes the five-step process is developed around a dialogue between a main character and a representative of a product or service. The representative may or may not be on camera. Live shots are used to fill in while the representative is talking. In the following example, note how the comments by the company representative follow a modified seven-step process.

VIDEO   AUDIO

STEP 1—SITUATION AND CHARACTERIZATION

FEMALE: (OPENING OUTSIDE DOOR
AND LETTING IN DOG.) HERE
COMES CHARLEY, AND THE
FLEAS.

---

3. Courtesy H. Taylor Lynn, District Manager, Residence Advertising, Southern Bell. Mike Brown, Tucker Wayne and Co., Advertising.

STEP 2—RISING ACTION

> FEMALE: I CAN GET THE FLEAS OFF
> CHARLEY, BUT WHAT ABOUT THE
> CARPET AND FURNITURE?

STEP 3—CLIMAX

> ANNCR: (VO) TRY NEW FLEA AND TICK
> KILLER BY RID-A-BUG. NO MORE
> MESSY AEROSOLS, EXPENSIVE
> EXTERMINATORS, OR FOGGERS
> THAT FORCE YOU OUT OF THE
> HOUSE. SPRAY RID-A-BUG ON
> FURNITURE AND CARPETING IN A
> FINE MIST. EVEN SPRAY
> CHARLEY'S BED. WHERE EVER
> THERE IS A FLEA PROBLEM. NO
> STAINS, NO ODORS.

STEP 4—FALLING ACTION

> FEMALE: NO TICKS, NO FLEAS!

STEP 5—DENOUEMENT

> ANNCR: (VO) NEW FLEA AND TICK
> KILLER FROM RID-A-BUG.[4]

Example 5

The following five-step dramatic commercial has a single setting and two characters. The character contrasts help make it an emotionally effective script.

VIDEO	AUDIO

STEP 1—SITUATION AND CHARACTERIZATION

GRANDFATHER AND GRANDAUGHTER SITTING SIDE BY SIDE LOOKING AT A PHOTO SCRAPBOOK.	GIRL: GRANDPA . . . WHAT DOES INSURANCE MEAN?

STEP 2—RISING ACTION

> GRAMPS: WELL . . . INSURANCE MEANS
> PROTECTING THE ONES YOU LOVE,

---

4. Courtesy Kenco Chemical and Manufacturing Corp., Jacksonville, Florida. Commercial prepared by Taylor Advertising, Inc.

                              AND ALSO THOSE THINGS THAT
                              ARE IMPORTANT TO YOU.

STEP 3—CLIMAX

                              GIRL: LIKE MOMMY AND DADDY?
                              GRAMPS: YEAH . . . LIKE MOMMY AND
                                 DADDY. YOU SEE, WHEN YOUR
                                 DADDY WAS YOUR AGE, YOUR
                                 GRANDMA AND I DECIDED TO
                                 INSURE THE FAMILY WITH A
                                 COMPANY WE COULD TRUST. A
                                 COMPANY THAT WOULD GROW, AS
                                 OUR NEEDS GREW. SO WE
                                 DECIDED TO INSURE WITH
                                 ROGER-ATKINS INSURANCE.

STEP 4—FALLING ACTION
GRAMPS, GIRL STILL SITTING.   GIRL: ROGERS-ATKINS?
                                  GRAMPS: YEP, CAUSE THEY'RE A
                                     COMPANY WE CAN TRUST. (HUGS
                                     HER. SHE HUGS HIM.)

STEP 5—DENOUEMENT

                              ANNCR: (VO) ROGER-ATKINS . . . "THE
                                 TRUST COMPANY."[5]

Using the Five-Step Process

Here is a procedure for writing the five-step process dramatic commercial.

  1. Accumulate adequate data about a product or service. Then develop a detailed fact sheet. Follow the same procedures you used in developing a fact sheet for the six-step and seven-step processes.
  2. Develop and write down the basic thesis, theme, or central idea as it relates to a problem, need, feeling, or desire.
  3. Devise and write down an appropriate plot sequence, a story line. If, after you have completed the story line, it does not seem appropriate or compatible with your thesis, theme, or central idea as it relates to a problem, need, feeling, or desire, then revise until there is compatibility. Occasionally you may need to start all over.

---

  5. Courtesy Duane Franceschi, President, Financial Marketing Concepts, Inc., Tallahassee, Florida.

4. Create the character(s) who will be involved in the plot. Write a detailed description of the character. If the character is not compatible, that is, if he or she conflicts with your product, service, or story, then revise and develop a character who is compatible.

5. Fill in the plot step by step. Be sure you have adequate conflicts so that the leading character(s) will have to make an effort to achieve the goal you have established. Remember, conflict (uncertainty) makes the story in a commercial interesting. Without conflict there can be no climax and therefore no resolution. Write your commercial first in narrative form, tucking in dialogue when you feel it or hear it.

6. Next, write the scenario. This is an exercise in shaping the commercial. It is best done scene by scene. Many writers use a storyboard during this step. Include all camera shots that relate to the plot. By following this procedure in your writing, each succeeding scene will grow out of the preceding scene. Be sure to end each scene (until the last one) with a touch of uncertainty, or conflict, to create a feeling of suspense. Suspense gives a commercial a feeling of continuity and makes it more exciting. Keep the excitement building to the climax.

7. Be sure the falling action and the denouement are adequate in that the leading character achieves a goal or is helped to achieve a goal related to the product.

8. Now, with the help of the five-step process, write the commercial. Do this step by step from the opening to the final scene. Essentially this task is one of turning the narrative you have developed into dialogue form. If the dialogue you have already written is adequate, use it. Change at this time is the nature of the writing procedure. In general, creativity is made to happen.

ASSIGNMENTS: THE FIVE-STEP DRAMATIC COMMERCIAL

1. Use the same fact sheets developed previously if you wish. However, if time permits, it will give you additional experience to develop new ones.

2. Write as many five-step process dramatic commercials of different lengths and types as your instructor feels time permits.

3. Make some of your commercials completely dramatic; in some, introduce narrators, demonstrators, or whomever you need.

4. Be sure to follow the five-step process in detail. Constantly write down what is needed in each step. Use a storyboard if you find it helpful. The object of these routines is to help you develop skill in writing the dramatic commercial.

PART III

REWRITING

CHAPTER 7

Rewriting

Copywriting is accomplished in three basic steps. The first step is *prewriting*—getting ready to write. The second step is *writing*—putting your copy together. The third step may be more important than these two steps combined. Most commercials get on the air because they have been finely tuned through *rewriting*.

There are many reasons why copy may need editing. Some of these reasons have been mentioned from time to time in the first two parts of this text. These reasons concern the various rules and regulations that govern broadcast communication. You will discover additional rules and regulations that relate to editing after you are on the job.

The most important reason for rewriting has to do with the basic theme of this book: *Writing can be learned*. Therefore, as a beginner, or as a person who wants to improve his or her writing technique, you need to keep in mind that while preparation for writing and actual writing are important, it is *rewriting* that may contribute most to your achieving the goal of becoming a professional copywriter.

Many editing procedures and techniques are in use today, but here are three approaches to rewriting that will help you.

QUESTIONS TO ASK WHILE REWRITING

- In the opening of this commercial, has interest in the thesis, theme, or central idea as it relates to a problem, need, feeling or desire been aroused?
- Is the overall structure of the script well conceived?
- Does the commercial depend on action scenes, or is it told by a narrator? Which is more appropriate for this commercial?
- Are all scenes absolutely necessary? Can some be combined or omitted?
- Does each scene cause the listener-viewer to stay tuned to the commercial to see how it turns out?
- Is all the action properly motivated?
- Are there double entendres, that is, double meanings? If there are, are they in keeping with the product or service being promoted in the commercial?
- Are there unconscious rhymes or repetitions in letter sounds that call attention to themselves and distract from what is meant?
- Is the script approximately the right length? If it is too long, what can be cut? If it is too short, where can it be lengthened?
- Have you used words with single meanings? If not, have you qualified those that have multimeanings?
- Did you leave out all words and ideas that are not relevant?
- Does what you have written fulfill the function and purpose of each process you followed?
- In a dramatic commercial, has the character(s) as well as the time or place been clearly established in the first scene?
- Does the plot proceed rapidly and surely from an interesting beginning to a major peak of interest at the climax?
- Is it clear and logical how and why the major character(s) becomes a person with a problem?
- Is it clear what the problem, need, feeling, or desire really is? Does the explanation occur early enough in the script?
- Are the obstacles that threaten to keep the leading character from getting what he or she wants clearly stated?
- Is the language in the dramatic commercial suitable and in keeping with the characterization, or did you impose dialect concepts on the character?
- Are the scenes too short or too long?
- When the character(s) moves from one scene to another, does the script make the need for the change clear?
- Is each scene worked out so that at all times it is clear where the character(s) is and why?

- Is each character sufficiently different and is each necessary to the scene?
- Are any of the character(s) speeches too long? Too short?

STRENGTHENING LANGUAGE WITH RHYTHM

The more speakable the language you write, the more meaningful your message is to the listener-viewer. When the meaning of a spoken message is rhythmical, it is usually more easily understood. As a result, it has a greater impact on the listener-viewer.

We all know that poetry has rhythm. That is what differentiates it from prose. But prose has rhythm too. Rhythm may be defined as the stream or flow of accented and unaccented syllables. In prose the pattern varies, although quality writing often approaches a rhythmic regularity that contributes to the listener-viewer's feeling of vigor and elation.[1] When this occurs, your prose will be empathically felt as well as understood. However, emotional appeal is also needed to strengthen the power of prose. It is this characteristic that dominates Walt Whitman's famous book *Leaves of Grass*. The opening lines of Lincoln's Gettysburg Address, because it is rhythmical and possesses imagery, also illustrate this basic phenomenon. Lincoln wrote: "Four score and seven years ago, our fathers brought forth upon this continent a new nation conceived in liberty and dedicated to the proposition that all men are created equal."

Another example of how rhythm and imagery can strengthen writing is Franklin D. Roosevelt's statement in his first inaugural address. He said, "The only thing we have to fear is fear itself." Note how the imagery, the emotional appeal, and the basic metric rhythm combine to turn that statement into language that is easily spoken, readily remembered, and deeply felt.

The rhythmic patterns used most of the time by professional writers are da-*dum*, da-da-*dum*, da-*dum*-dum. The basic pattern is da-*dum*. The accent is on the second syllable. There are, however, more words in our language that are rhythmically *dum*-da. The accent is on the first syllable. Nonetheless, the da-*dum* melody in our language is universally used. Because of this, most writers introduce *dum*-da words with a one-syllable word, an article, or a preposition. For example, the word *writing* is rhythmically *dum*-da. To change the rhythm, start the sentence with a preposition as follows: In writing (da-*dum*-da), when writing (da-*dum*-da), if writing (da-*dum*-da), and so on, "In writing a letter to you." Professional writers do this because a predominance of da-*dum*, da-da-*dum*, and

---

1. John Diamond, M.D., *Behavioral Kinesiology* (New York: Harper & Row, 1979).

da-*dum-dum* accents in a sentence causes it to end on an accented syllable. When this occurs, the sentence is considered to be stronger and therefore more dynamic. Any statement that uses a predominance of *dum*-da, *dum-dum*-da, or *dum*-da-da accents is weak, and therefore less dynamic.

The following statements were taken off the air. Note how each one ends in an accented beat of da-*dum*, da-da-*dum*, or da-*dum-dum*. This rhythm helps each statement sound positive.

LET DIALING FOR DOLLARS GIVE YOUR PURSE A SILVER LINING.

NOW TAKE THE PRESSURE OUT OF RUSH HOUR WITH THE JONNIE SHOW.

HAROLD SMITH HAS BETTER WEATHER 'CAUSE HE HELPS YOU UNDERSTAND.

The statements that follow end on an unstressed beat of *dum*-da. As a result they tend to confuse the message and turn-off the listener-viewer. Each sentence also begins with an accented syllable.

DON'T LET YOUR DEBTS UPSET YOU.

PLAY-BY-PLAY BASEBALL WITH RONALD HART STICKS THE BALL AND BAT IN YOUR EAR.

LISTEN TO WXYZ FOR NEWS THAT'S THE LATEST.

Dum-da and *dum*-da-da vocal rhythms are habitually used by individuals who feel weak and insecure about themselves. Listener-viewers hearing these rhythms in language tend to respond negatively about that which is being said.[2]

One of the useful ways to understand how rhythm is used in language is to tape a quality network commercial and study the melody of its language. Be sure to use a network commercial. Transcribe the text on paper, and as you play the recording over and over, study and mark the rhythm.

USING TRANSITIONAL WORDS AND PHRASES

A single statement rarely communicates a satisfactory message to a listener-viewer. All single statements need help. Transitional words and phrases help one idea flow smoothly to the next. They are an excellent

2. J. Clark Weaver and Richard J. Anderson, "Voice and Personality Interrelationships," *Southern Speech Communication Journal* 38 (1973): 262–78.

writing technique. Their use will help you achieve singleness of purpose and add reinforcement to your writing.

The most useful transitional words and phrases for the copywriter are identified as *internal*. Internal transitional words and phrases help create a smooth flow of language in the development of an idea. They do this by guiding the mind and the emotions of the listener-viewer from one idea to the next. There are several ways this process is developed.

The subject of a sentence may be repeated   The subject of a previous sentence, the main word or group of words denoting that which is affirmed or predicated, may be repeated in the sentence that follows. Repeating the noun turns it into an internal transition and is an ideal way to achieve emphasis by repetition. The following examples illustrate the usefulness of this procedure as a writing technique.

ACME IS AN EFFICIENT MOVER. ACME IS A DEPENDABLE MOVER.

ADOLPH'S MEAT TENDERIZER IS MEAT INSURANCE. WITH ADOLPH'S YOU CAN BE SURE YOU'RE GETTING THE MOST OUT OF YOUR CUT OF MEAT.

ANACIN HAS THE PAIN RELIEVER DOCTORS RECOMMEND MOST. ANACIN WILL GET RID OF YOUR HEADACHE FAST.

BOUNTY SOAKS UP SPILLS FASTER THAN ANY OTHER BRAND. BOUNTY, THE QUICKER PICKER-UPPER.

CERTS IS A BREATH MINT. CERTS IS A CANDY MINT.

COKE ADDS LIFE. COKE! IT'S THE REAL THING.

DOUBLEMINT GUM DOUBLES YOUR PLEASURE, DOUBLEMINT GUM IS DOUBLY GOOD.

DRY IDEAL CONTAINS ONLY THIS MUCH WATER. DRY IDEAL CAN GO ON DRY AND KEEP YOU DRY.

ECKERDS GIVES YOU TWICE THE PRINTS. ECKERDS GIVE YOU TWICE THE FILM.

FRED FARBER AND ASSOCIATES DO GOOD WORK. FRED FARBER AND ASSOCIATES ARE PROFESSIONAL.

STARKIST DOESN'T WANT TUNA WITH GOOD TASTE. STARKIST WANTS TUNA THAT TASTES GOOD.

RAID, THE FASTEST OF ANY ROACH KILLER. RAID KILLS BUGS DEAD.

The central idea or key words may be repeated in the succeeding sentence   The technique for accomplishing this form of repetition is to take the object of the first sentence, that which is being talked about, and use it as the subject of the second sentence. The noun equivalent in a verb construction may also be used.

> SCOTTIES OFFERS YOU A SELECTION OF BEAUTIFUL DECORATER BOXES. THESE BOXES HELP ADD PRETTINESS AND WARMTH TO ANY ROOM IN THE HOUSE.

> LISTERMINT KEEPS YOUR BREATH FEELING CLEAN ALL DAY. AND CLEAN BREATH CAN MAKE ALL THE DIFFERENCE.

> LOOK FOR THE SEAL OF COTTON. THE MORE COTTON THE BETTER YOU FEEL.

> SCAN DESIGN CARRIES DANISH FURNITURE. DANISH FURNITURE MAKES YOUR HOUSE A HOME.

> LIFEBUOY CONTAINS A BRAND-NEW DEODORANT. A DEODORANT THAT KEEPS ON WORKING.

> IF YOU DRINK, DON'T DRIVE. IF YOU DRIVE, DON'T DRINK.

> SOUTHERN BREAD BELIEVES IN FRESHNESS. FRESHNESS THAT LASTS AND LASTS.

> FINAL-NET REALLY HOLDS UP. IT HOLDS UP EVEN BETTER THAN YOU DO.

> MRS. KINSEY'S HOMEMADE PIES ARE FROZEN. ALTHOUGH THEY'RE FROZEN, WHEN YOU BAKE THEM YOU'LL FIND THEY TASTE OVEN FRESH.

> EDUCATION IS THE KEY TO KNOWLEDGE. KNOWLEDGE IS THE KEY TO UNDERSTANDING AND WISDOM.

> PUBLIX, WHERE SHOPPING IS A PLEASURE. AND THE PLEASURE'S ALL YOURS.

> AMNITY WALLETS ARE MADE OF TOUGH LEATHER. THIS TOUGH LEATHER IS MADE TO LAST AND LAST.

A pronoun reference may be used as an internal transition A *pronoun* is a word used instead of, or in place of, a noun. A pronoun is one of a small number of words referring to a person, place, or thing that is either named, asked for, or understood in the context of what is being said. The use of a pronoun reference as an internal transition is achieved by substituting a pronoun for the main noun in the second sentence. However, the relationship between the pronoun and its referent, its meaning, must be unmistakable. When the meaning is clear, the use of a pronoun reference is a helpful writing technique.

TEST DRIVE A VOLVO. IT MAY SURPRISE YOU.

CHOOSE KEEPSAKE CHINA. IT GIVES YOUR TABLE THAT CLASSIC TOUCH.

BUY PSYCHOLOGY TODAY. IT MAY CHANGE YOUR PERSPECTIVE ON LIFE.

BUY YOUR CHILD SOME PLAY-DOUGH. IT MAY OPEN UP A NEW WORLD OF CREATIVITY.

TASTER'S CHOICE IS ONE HUNDRED PERCENT FREEZE DRIED COFFEE. IT LOOKS, SMELLS, AND TASTES LIKE GROUND ROAST COFFEE.

SECRET DEODORANT IS FOR WOMEN. IT SMELLS PRETTY.

HANDLE WITH CARE DOES MORE. IT CLEANS BODY SOIL BETTER.

OUR LOTION MAKES SKIN LOOK FRESHER AND HEALTHIER. IT ACTS AS A GUARD.

A CRICKET LIGHTER IS REALLY QUITE A LIGHT. IT WILL LAST FOR MONTHS AND STILL BURN BRIGHT.

TRY CALVERT EXTRA. IT MAKES YOUR DRINK SOFT.

A SUBARU CAN SAVE YOU MONEY. IT'S ESTIMATED AT FORTY-THREE MILES PER GALLON ON THE HIGHWAY, TWENTY-NINE IN THE CITY.

PERET'S MILK IS DELICIOUS. IT'S FARM FRESH.

Parallel structure As a writing technique, *parallel structure* can improve the quality of your writing. It uses an idea in one sentence and then compares or contrasts it with another idea. Parallel structure is achieved by including in the second sentence a phrase similar to the phrase contained in the first. Some of the ways that parallel structure can be used are in the following examples:

WHEN YOU USE ARM AND HAMMER BAKING SODA IN YOUR REFRIGERATOR, YOU'LL NOTICE FEWER ODORS. WHEN YOU USE ARM AND HAMMER BAKING SODA IN YOUR PASTRIES, YOU'LL NOTICE FLAKY CRUSTS.

BEER MAKES IT GOOD. SCHLITZ MAKES IT GREAT.

USE BIC STREAMLINE FOR A FINER POINT PEN. USE BIC BOLD FOR A WIDER POINT PEN.

BURDINE'S JEWELERS PUT MORE SPARKLE IN YOUR EYES. BURDINE'S JEWELERS ALSO PUT LESS BIND ON YOUR BUDGET.

DUBONET'S PARLOR HAS A SALAD BAR FOR THOSE WHO WANT TO

LOSE WEIGHT. IT ALSO HAS AN ICE-CREAM BAR FOR THOSE WHO
WANT TO GAIN WEIGHT.

JOIN AN ADVENTURE. JOIN THE NAVY.

YOUR SKIN LOOKS INCREDIBLE. YOUR SKIN FEELS MOIST WHEN THE
AIR IS DRY.

SHE SAYS YES TO LIFE. VAN REALTY SAYS YES TO THAT.

WESTINGHOUSE WASHERS MAKE WASHING EASIER. WESTINGHOUSE
WASHERS MAKE WASHING COST LESS.

Enumeration   As a writing technique, *enumeration* employs various devices. These devices are used to achieve a smooth transition from one sentence to the next. As a writer, you may develop enumerative devices by stating that a particular number of items or events exist. Then you may count them one at a time, tell of, or about one event after another, or give a listing item by item. The following sentences illustrate various ways that enumeration may be developed.

THE PINTO SAVES YOU MONEY TWO WAYS. FIRST, IT COST LESS.
SECOND, IT USES LESS GAS.

TWO THINGS MAKE ZENITH TELEVISION BETTER. NUMBER ONE, ITS
REPUTATION FOR DEPENDABILITY. NUMBER TWO, ITS QUINTRIX
PICTURE.

BETTY CROCKER OFFERS THREE SUGGESTIONS FOR ORGANIZED AND
EFFICIENT COOKERY. FIRST, KEEP A FILE BOX OF RECIPES UNDER
DIVISIONS OF ENTREES, VEGETABLES, BREAD, SALAD, AND DESERT.
SECOND, STORE KITCHEN UTENSILS IN SIMILAR GROUPINGS.
ACCORDING TO THEIR USE. THIRD, PLAN MENUS BEFORE YOU GO
SHOPPING SO YOU CAN ESTABLISH NEED ITEMS BEFOREHAND.

BEECH'S SHAMPOO MAKES TWO PROMISES. FIRST, YOUR HAIR WILL
HAVE MORE BODY. SECOND, YOUR HAIR WILL BE CONDITIONED.

THIS POT IS MADE IN THREE STEPS. FIRST, IT IS MOLDED. NEXT, IT IS
FIRED. LAST, IT IS GLAZED.

THREE BASIC APPEALS TO MANKIND ARE USED IN COPYWRITING. THE
FIRST IS LOGIC, THE SECOND IS ETHIC, THE THIRD IS EMOTION.

THERE ARE THREE WAYS TO CHANGE YOUR HAIR COLOR. FIRST, GET
THE NEIGHBOR TO DO IT. SECOND, DO IT YOURSELF. THIRD, LET THE
SUBURBAN SALON GIVE YOU THE PROFESSIONAL ATTENTION YOU CAN
TRUST.

TWO STEPS CAN HELP GET RID OF YOUR COLD. FIRST, DRINK JUICES.
SECOND, GET PLENTY OF SLEEP.

Addition   As a copywriting device, *addition* is a means by which a
thought may be expanded. This technique uses certain words, or word
combinations, with which to attach an additional meaning or unit of
thought to a previous one. The use of this technique will help you
supplement the main idea or thought.

The words that follow may be used to introduce or relate additional
meanings. The serious writer will discover many more.

again	continuous	moreover
also	further	next
along	furthermore	plus
and	included	subsequently
another	including	then
besides	last	therefore
consequently	likewise	too

The phrases that follow are often used by copywriters in developing
supplemental thoughts and meanings. There are many other such phrases.

added to	as well as
along the same	at the same time
an additional	of equal importance
another important	in addition
another point	in conjunction with
another related	not only

The following sentences illustrate some of the many ways that addition
as a technique may be used by a writer.

BESIDES THAT, YOUR TIRES WILL BE CHECKED.

FURTHERMORE, OUR MENU INCLUDES A FREE BEVERAGE OF YOUR
CHOICE.

INCLUDED ARE THE TOP PARTY SONGS IN THE RADIO FORMAT.

MOREOVER, YOU MAY ADD ADDITIONAL MILK TO THE MIXTURE TO
MAKE IT THINNER.

NOT ONLY ARE THE NEW HOURS CONVENIENT, BUT WE'RE ALSO
OFFERING NEW BENEFITS TO OUR EMPLOYEES.

NOT ONLY DOES GARFIELD'S GROCERY MARKET PROVIDE PERSONAL
SERVICE, IT DELIVERS TO YOUR HOME.

TO ADD TO THE PASSENGERS' ENJOYMENT THE SHIP WILL HOLD
SEVERAL COMPETITIVE EVENTS INCLUDING A SWIMMING MATCH.

EX-LAX ALSO WORKS WITH YOUR SYSTEM'S NATURAL BODY FLUIDS.

Clarification   As a copywriting technique, clarification employs the use of certain words singly and in combination to help make what is being said more easily and more clearly communicated. Clarification is the process of giving an example and referring to something that is similar.

The following words, word combinations, and phrases are often used by professional copywriters to introduce additional explanation for clarifying a thought. There are many others.

an explanation of this	as a matter of fact
clearly	evidently
in essence	in explanation
in fact	in other words
for example	for the purpose of understanding
that is	that is to say
this means	by that is meant
to be more explicit	to be more precise
to clarify	to demonstrate
to illustrate	said another way
specifically	what I mean is

The following sentences illustrate some of the ways that the principle of clarification may be used within a paragraph.

BREVITY, AS HAS BEEN POINTED OUT, IS THE KEY TO PRECISENESS.

IN EXPLANATION, THESE BRIGHT COLORS FIT THE MOOD OF THE
PARTY MUCH BETTER.

TO CLARIFY, A DIAMOND WAS ONCE A PIECE OF COAL THAT WENT
THROUGH INTENSE HEAT AND PRESSURE FOR REFINEMENT.

TO CONVINCE YOURSELF, WASH YOUR DISHES WITH THIS DETERGENT
AND NOTE THE REDUCTION IN SPOTTING.

TO EXPLAIN WHY THIS CAR IS TRULY BETTER, IT HAS A CRUISE
CONTROL FOR A MORE RELAXED DRIVE.

TO ILLUSTRATE, LET US COMPARE THIS NEW PACKAGE DESIGN WITH
OUR OLD ONE.

Comparison   As a writing technique, *comparison* employs the use of certain words to bring two or more objects, thoughts, persons, or events together within a paragraph. This is done for the purpose of noting their likenesses. The use of comparison as a writing technique helps clarify or emphasize the resemblances.

The following words, word combinations, and phrases represent a few of the ways that comparison as a technique may be used.

also	in a like manner
analogy	in comparison
analogous to this	in the same way
a related point is	it is, moreover
as	keeping this in mind
comparatively	like
corresponding to this	like the previous point
equivalent	on the same note
identical	representative
in a similar way	similarily
imitation of	similar

The following sentences represent a few of the ways that comparison as a copywriting technique may be used.

THIS VACATION PLAN ALSO INCLUDES A WEEK'S STAY IN VIENNA.

SIMILARILY, THIS BOOK IS A DOOR TO KNOWLEDGE.

COMPARATIVELY, THE VOLKSWAGEN GETS MORE MILES PER GALLON AND HAS FEWER MAINTENANCE COSTS THAN ANY OTHER CAR IN AMERICA.

THESE TWO UNITS OF THE SYSTEM MATCH PERFECTLY.

THERE IS NO PARALLEL TO THIS KIND OF BARGAIN.

THIS PRODUCT IS IDENTICAL BUT COSTS LESS.

YOU SHOULD FEED YOUR CAT IN THE SAME WAY YOU FEED YOUR FAMILY. WITH LOVE AND CARE.

LIKE ALL PRODUCTS MADE BY SEARS, THIS TOASTER IS DEPENDABLE.

Contrast   As a copywriting technique, *contrast* employs the use of certain words or phrases to indicate the difference between two or more objects, persons, thoughts, or events. The use of contrast makes these differences clearer to the listener-viewer.

The following words, word combinations, and phrases represent a few of the many ways that the principle of contrast may be stated.

although	but
despite	however
neither	still
unlike	yet
conversely	dissimilarily
after all	at the same time
for all that	if not
in contrast	instead of
inspite of	nevertheless
notwithstanding	on the contrary
on the one hand	on the other hand

The following sentences illustrate some of the ways that contrast as a technique may be used to clarify an idea.

ALTHOUGH HE IS YOUNGER, POLITICALLY HE IS MORE EXPERIENCED.

THIS MATERIAL IS STRONG, BUT THIN.

YOUR DOG MAY EAT ALL THE TABLE SCRAPS YOU PUT BEFORE HIM, BUT THEY WILL NOT PROVIDE HIM WITH THE VITAMINS HE REALLY NEEDS.

OTHER SCHOOLS FOLLOW THE SEMESTER SYSTEM. THIS SCHOOL FOLLOWS THE QUARTER SYSTEM.

MAKE YOUR CHOICE TODAY. DON'T WAIT UNTIL TOMORROW.

HE IS THE BETTER CANDIDATE IN SPITE OF HIS INEXPERIENCE.

A DIAMOND IS NOT JUST FOR NOW. IT IS FOREVER.

IN CONTRAST, THE LACK OF MONEY CAN CREATE PROBLEMS.

UNLIKE MOST WOMEN WHO SEW THEIR OWN, YOUR CLOTHES REFLECT YOUR PERSONALITY.

IT'S INGENIOUS. IT'S GENUINE BELL.

Exemplification As a copywriting technique, *exemplification* is accomplished through the use of a word, or words in combination, by introducing an example or an explanation that will illustrate a previous statement. Exemplification is used to develop greater clarity and increase comprehension.

The following words and word combinations represent a few of the ways that exemplification as a writing technique may be used.

exhibits	exemplifies
indicates	shows

| a case in point | as the instructions state |
| as the statement implies | for example |

The following sentences are ways in which the principle of exemplification as a writing technique is used to develop clarification.

THIS HOUSE IS AN EXAMPLE OF COLONIAL ARCHITECTURE.

AS THE INSTRUCTIONS STATE, SNIFF PROOF SAVES YOU EMBARRASSMENT FROM THE SMELL OF FRIED FOODS, CIGARETTE SMOKE, AND OTHER COLD WEATHER ODORS.

AS YOU KNOW, THE CESSNA AIRPLANE COSTS LESS, YET THE RIDE IS SMOOTHER AND THE CABIN ROOMIER THAN MOST FOUR-SEATER PLANES.

FOR EXAMPLE, THIS TAPE TURNED YELLOW IN A YEAR. THIS SCOTCH BRAND TAPE REMAINS CLEAR.

NATURE'S WAY POLISH CLEANS YOUR WOOD SURFACES WITHOUT LEAVING A BUILD-UP.

HABIT CALLS FOR A NEW WAY OF CELEBRATING THANKSGIVING. SMITH'S FROZEN TURKEY PIES.

LET ME SAY YOUR HUSBAND FEELS ABOUT HIS KAWASAKI THE WAY YOU FEEL ABOUT YOUR SOAP OPERAS.

THE BEST BEER FOR THE TIME OF THE DAY.

Place   As a writing technique, *place* is the use of words and phrases that designate a specific location. The use of place is helpful in creating visual imagery. It is achieved by using an appropriate noun, verb, adjective, adverb, or combination to explain the physical location of a person, place, object, occasion, circumstance, or context in relation to an event or situation.

The following words indicate ways that place as a copywriting technique may be indicated. The use of place is helpful in classifying an idea's relationship in terms of *where* and *how*.

after	across	above	among
area	around	at	behind
below	down	before	everywhere
by	centrally	elsewhere	near
here	inside	midway	over
nearly	neighborhood	outside	opposite
past	somewhere	someplace	spot
there	underneath	whereabouts	within

The following sentences illustrate a few ways by which place may be classified in terms of *where* and *how*.

AVOID THAT SCRATCHY FEELING IN YOUR THROAT.

STORE DEAD-ALL BENEATH YOUR KITCHEN SINK.

PLACE THIS PAD BENEATH YOUR COFFEE POT.

FOR SALE AT ALL MAJOR DRUG STORES.

POISONS SHOULD BE PLACED BEYOND THE REACH OF CHILDREN.

JUST SPRAY IT IN THE AIR AND ODORS WILL DISAPPEAR.

HERE COMES WRANGLER AND HE HAS THE ANSWER ON HIS POCKET.

STOP THAT THROBBING FEELING INSIDE YOUR HEAD.

JUST SPRAY IT ON THE GREASY SPOT AND CLEAN WILL DO THE REST.

SPRAY THIS LOTION ON YOUR HANDS AND FEEL THE DIFFERENCE.

Qualification   As a writing technique, *qualification* means that the writer modifies an attribute, statement, concept, idea, or restricts the condition essential to understanding, accepting, or believing it. The use of such qualifying words or phrases helps the writer develop specificity.

The following words, when used appropriately, help restrict or limit the meaning of an initial statement so that it is more readily understood. In this way, qualifying words are helpful in developing idea relationships in terms of *why*. There are many others available.

apparently	clearly	conceivably
considering	evidently	hopefully
maybe	obviously	perhaps
possible	possibly	plainly
presumably	seemingly	slightly
somewhat	unfortunately	willingly

Qualifying phrases are especially useful in restricting or limiting the meaning of a statement. Examples:

according to	as far as one can judge by appearances
based on	because of
for certain	in anticipation of
I am sure that	I feel without a doubt
it can be assumed that	it may be that
it is reasonable that	logically speaking
without a doubt	when everything is considered

The following sentences illustrate some of the ways that *qualification* as a writing technique may be employed.

IF THERE IS A LACK OF SPACE IN YOUR APARTMENT, CHOOSE FROM OUR SELECTION OF BAMBOO ATTACHED SHELVES.

CLEARLY, TRAVELING BY NORTHEAST AIR IS THE QUICKEST WAY TO TRANSACT BUSINESS WHEN COMPARED WITH OTHER AIRLINE TRAVEL.

OBVIOUSLY LEMON JOY LIQUID CUTS GREASE BETTER THAN OTHER LEADING BRANDS.

PLAINLY RICHMAN BROTHERS WANTS TO CUSTOM FIT YOUR CLOTHING AND CATER YOUR WARDROBE NEEDS.

WHEN YOU CONSIDER THE COST THERE IS NO ALTERNATIVE.

ACCORDING TO THE MONEY MARKET, NOW IS THE TIME TO BUY.

MAYBE YOU'LL FIND A NEW WAY TO USE ARM AND HAMMER BAKING SODA.

WITHOUT A DOUBT YOU'LL LOVE IT TOO.

THE MORE COST EFFICIENT, THE BETTER THE SHOE.

CLEARLY HEALTH-SUPPORT IS THE BETTER BUY.

Reference As a copywriting technique, the use of *reference* means that the writer chooses a word, word combination, or phrase to point out a specified meaning. The use of reference helps the copywriter call the listener-viewer's attention to a specific statement, passage, point, condition, circumstance, person, place, or thing. Reference is used to indicate how a statement or remark may have a bearing on the subject or problem being discussed. The following words are useful in helping fulfill a point of reference.

everyone	here	he	it
many	other	that	them
there	these	this	those
she	whatever	where	which

The following word combinations and phrases are often used by writers as a reference.

associated with	everyone who
concerned with	in accordance with
in the case of	in reference to
that which	one that

        the one who   the person who
        with regard to

The following sentences illustrate some of the ways that reference as a writing technique may be developed.

THIS ENCYCLOPEDIA CAN BE USED BY EVERYONE IN THE FAMILY.

RON BROWN WILL BE AT DUBEY'S BOOKSTORE THIS AFTERNOON. HE WILL AUTOGRAPH A NOVEL FOR YOU.

CURRENTLY YOU CANNOT FIND A BETTER BUY.

THE ONE YOU CAN ALWAYS TRUST IS BEACHUM BABY FOOD.

THERE YOU WILL FIND THE SOUTHWOOD SHOPPING PLAZA.

THIS CAN BE THE BEST BUY YOU'LL MAKE THIS YEAR.

THOSE, YOUR DOCTOR WILL TELL YOU, ARE SYMPTOMS OF THE COMMON COLD.

WHATEVER POLICY YOU BUY WE'RE HERE TO BACK YOU.

AT DATSUN WE ARE DRIVEN.

Summary   As a copywriting technique, *summary* is a means used to recapitulate, review, reexamine, reiterate, or sum up that which has been stated or implied. Generally the copywriter's use of this technique is for the purpose of forming a conclusion in a concise and orderly fashion. The following words are helpful in making a summary statement.

accordingly	as a result	as a quick summary
in brief	in capsule	in closing
in conclusion	in a few words	in a nutshell
in review	in short	in summary
on the whole	to close	to recapitulate
to reiterate	to repeat	to sum up

The following sentences illustrate a few of the ways that summary may be used.

AFTER ALL IS SAID AND DONE, THIS DRINK APPEALS TO THE EIGHTEEN TO THIRTY-FOUR AGE GROUP.

IN BRIEF, THE MOVIE IS ONE YOU'LL LOVE TO SEE.

WE BELIEVE YOU'LL WANT TO BUILD YOUR HOME IN HOLLYHILLS.

TO REPEAT, WE DON'T KNOW OF A BETTER BUY.

BULLWINKLE'S FINAL REMINDER IS, STUDY NOW AND PARTY LATER.

IN BRIEF, YOU CANNOT BUY A BETTER CAR.

IN SHORT, YOU'LL BE GLAD YOU DID.

I NORMALLY DON'T GO AROUND CHATTERING ABOUT COMFORT.

Time   The use of a word that indicates some relationship to *time* is often a helpful copywriting technique. A word referring to time defines or specifies the period during which something has or will take place. Such words imply the succession of events with regard to a given period.

The following words, plus many others, are used to indicate one of the several instances during which the element of time is a factor in correlating that which is being said or described as belonging to the period within which it transpires.

after	afterward	before	continually
currently	during	earlier	finally
formerly	immediately	past	lately
later	meanwhile	next	now
past	presently	recently	since
shortly	soon	simultaneously	subsequently
temporarily	thereupon	today	throughout
until	while	yesterday	tomorrow

Phrases that indicate time are particularly useful to a writer wishing to indicate, identify, or describe various aspects of an event or occasion.

after a while	after a short time
at last	at that time
at the same time	a short time ago
at this moment	before now
from that time until now	continually afterward
identical moment	in the course of history
in the past	shortly after
until then	when its over

The following sentences illustrate some of the ways that time may be used.

WE WARN OUR CLIENTS BEFOREHAND OF ALL SUCH STIPULATIONS IN THE CONTRACT.

SEE YOUR DOCTOR TODAY, NOT AFTER THE EMERGENCY HAS OCCURRED.

DON'T WAIT UNTIL TOMORROW. PESKY BUGS KILLS BUGS DEAD NOW.

HAVE YOU BECOME INDIFFERENT LATELY?

WHY WAIT UNTIL LATER? DESIGNER JEANS ARE HERE TODAY.

CURRENTLY WE HAVE HUNDREDS OF STRAIGHT-LEGGED JEANS
AVAILABLE.

UNTIL THEN, SO LONG. SEE YOU TOMORROW.

THE SECOND TERM OF THE YEAR IS ALMOST OVER. RENT NEXT YEAR'S
APARTMENT, NOW.

INVEST NOW, BEFORE THE ECONOMY SHIFTS INTO A RECESSION.

Transitional words and phrases are useful tools with which to write commercial copy. Listen to how such words and phrases are used by professionals and then practice to develop your own way of having transitions work for you.

CONCLUSION

At some time in the future, after you have had considerable writing experience, you may begin adding and deleting writing procedures as you discover and understand how to write without wasting energy and time. Experience indicates that most successful writers add and delete many procedural techniques before intuition begins to take over and they settle down to their way of writing.

You will discover too that a top commercial, whether it is for radio, television, or both, is rarely ever the product of inspiration. Writing, like most human endeavor, is the product of hard work, patience, and a belief in your ability backed by know-how and physical stamina. For just as any top athlete improves his or her ability by thought, concentration, exacting repetition, and practice in an effort to become more efficient, similarly most writers improve their ability to write.

Naturally, most commercial writers hope to achieve a status of creativity. Use of the processes has helped many along the way. Their use has also been found to be a helpful apprenticeship by which you learn about other kinds of writing. Some copywriters turn to the documentary or to film. Some even turn to short stories, novels, and plays. The ability to write well has to be learned in each medium. In the final analysis, nothing helps more than self-discipline and disciplined writing. That is the way most writers "pay their dues" and prepare themselves to become professionals.

Index